WHAT MATTERS MOST
A Young Adult's Roadmap for Life

by A. J. Wasserstein

This book has been through editing, copyediting and proofing. I have read this book too many times. Despite multiple rounds of proofing and editing, there might still be some errors enclosed, which are my responsibility.

Printed in the United States of America
First Printing, 2017
ISBN 978-1-5464665-6-7
Summit Press
Summit Press Publishers
Canton, Connecticut
860-306-4057 Phone
www.summit-success.com

Cover Design and Interior Design by Chris Derrick

CONTENTS

SECTION 3:
WHAT MATTERS MOST

For Michael, Jake, and Leah
No words could ever describe just how much I love you.
Although Michael graduating from high school catalyzed
this book, it is a gift to each of you.

INTRODUCTION

June 2016

Dear Michael:

As I write, it is the summer of 2016; you've just completed your junior year of high school. It's such a cliché, but time has really zipped by and I cannot believe, in one year, you will leave for college.

I so distinctly remember bringing you home from Waterbury Hospital in November of 1998. It's hard to describe the emotions and feelings of parenthood until you actually experience them for yourself. Seventeen years ago, I was excited, nervous, overwhelmed, and hopeful; hopeful that you would become everything you wanted to be and live a happy and purposeful life.

A child leaving for college is a milestone for everybody in a family. You are about to embark on your own path and build your life. Our family dynamic will change at home and rebalance. This is the natural course, and although it's bitter-sweet in so many ways, it's to be and unavoidable.

Throughout your seventeen years, I've tried to be a role model and impart advice and wisdom—with mixed results, I suspect. I'm not sure how much was absorbed, but I hope some things were internalized, either explicitly or subliminally.

Despite my endless attempts to discuss many topics with you, I probably missed some conversations that would help you with the choices and challenges you're about to face. I thought it would be useful for you to have a roadmap to life—a codification of many things we have discussed and some I wish we had discussed—as you enter the next chapter of life. Like any map, it's your choice to follow, reject, or modify. I do not share these thoughts, this map, as a mandate; rather, I share them as things I wish I had known when I was your age, eons ago.

When I was beginning my own life of independence, I wish I had possessed such a map to follow, one that high-lighted some of the topics here. I, of course, have made many mistakes and perhaps some of them were more easily avoided. Maybe some of the lessons I've learned can be useful to you.

You're at an interesting age right now: clearly not a child anymore, yet not fully an adult. What's slightly challenging about this in-between stage is you might think you're an all-knowing experienced adult; and I might be guilty of still thinking of you as a little boy. Neither is true. You know far more than I likely understand, but perhaps less than you think.

When I was seventeen, I thought I was pretty smart; my father, on the other hand, didn't know very much. Well, I was wrong on both accounts. I didn't know anything; and my dad knew far more than I could ever understand—something that took me years to discover.

It wouldn't surprise me if you feel the same.

It might be hard for you to believe, but many of the decisions you make and the steps you take in the next decade will create the foundation of your next fifty years. Most young adults, including me, often make important decisions without perspective, guidance, context, or a complete understanding of implications. I hope this book better prepares you with a framework to make the best possible decisions for you and your path towards happiness.

So, the thoughts enclosed here are offered with the advantage of time and perspective, both of which you currently lack, but will gain. I'm just trying to share with you the very things I wish I'd had in my immature head when I was a young adult. The trick for you is to at least be open to the concept that there are things you don't yet know or understand—and that's a very hard notion to embrace when you feel invincible at seventeen!

As Rod Stewart famously crooned, "I wish I knew then what I know now."

This book will also help you get to know me in a deeper, and perhaps, different way. You see me as a father, a role I relish playing, but you might not fully understand the path I have travelled; what good choices I have made, and what poor choices I have also made. Don't worry, this isn't autobiographical at all, but I will share some examples of where I have gotten it right, and where I got it wrong. Hopefully, this will let you see me as an imperfect person, just like you, who struggled with many challenges along the way.

To help me with this book, I interviewed approximately 50 people. I wanted to get a diverse set of views and opinions to spare you from only hearing my voice. (I thought it would be helpful to engage some folks smarter than me.) The conversations I had were fascinating. The interactions were genuine and I truly enjoyed how people opened up and were so insightful, honest, vulnerable, and reflective. The chats were wide ranging and touched on many of the topics enclosed here, but centered on five key questions:

- What's the best advice you received as a young adult

starting your independent life? What do you wish you knew at 20 that you know now?

- What did you care a lot about at 20, that you now realize just didn't matter that much?

- What have you tried to teach or share with your own kids as they begin to embark on their own independent lives?

- What do you wish you shared with or taught your own kids, but missed?

- If you could provide a young adult with a "magic card"—one that would empower the recipient with the ability to make one life decision perfectly—for what would you hope it would be used?

I have organized this book by topic; the very ones I think will matter a great deal to you at some point. There are three broad sections . . .

In the first, we examine the big decisions: marriage, career, and where to live; also, dating, money, drugs, and alcohol—topics that can easily trip people up, starting in college.

In the second section, the most important in many ways, we look at who you are: how your values and virtues feed your character—as well as the difference between resume and eulogy virtues. We'll also explore the ultimate goal (happiness) and what often gets in the way (failure).

In the final section, I cover what matters most in life: relationships, finding your place in a bigger context, and serving your community.

Throughout these pages, I'll share my thoughts and perspectives and other viewpoints. But all of this is only for you to contemplate and consider; it's not intended to be prescriptive in telling you what to do specifically.

When you consider the content in this book, do not be tempted to think I have everything figured out. I absolutely do not. Even at fifty, I'm trying to be a better person, trying to figure things out myself. You will likely also spend a lifetime in that mode. It's OK to be imperfect; it's OK to work on getting better.

Raising you has been a labor of love, Michael—of purpose, of connection, of fulfillment.

Once, when you were about four years old and your brother, Jake, was three, Mom and I went upstairs to give you two your nightly bath. Working off a divide and conquer strategy, Mom took you, and I took Jake. As I began to ready Jake by undressing him and preparing the bath, he said, with great power in his voice, "I do not want you to be my worker!"

"What do you mean by being your 'worker'?" I asked.

Jake, always quick to make his opinions known, asserted, "You know, the person that works for you and does the bath and pajamas!"

I laughed. What an interesting perspective. Sometimes it did feel like work, taking care of your needs, serving you on my knees; but really, what better work is possible?

As you got older I would often joke that I was your chauffeur and ATM machine; shuttling you from activity to activity, sharing time in the car, and paying for your myriad of events. I have since been dislocated, now that you can drive. And although I'm still the ATM machine, I know that, too, will end shortly as you move on to self-sufficiency.

I have enjoyed being your worker, your chauffeur, and your ATM machine—I've enjoyed being your dad. Spending time with Mom, you, Jake, and Leah is the best, even if it isn't always smooth and perfect.

I've spoken with you many times about unconditional love. I truly believe the purest form of love is from a parent to a child. You don't need to do anything for me to love you; my love just is, in a pure and unadulterated form. I want the very best for you and want your life to be whatever you want it to be. Unconditional love is not contingent on anything you do. It's because of who you are.

I say this because I want you to understand that you're free to follow your own path. You're free to take my advice, or leave it. The thoughts laid out on the following pages are not intended to shape you in any way, just to give you the tools and options to blaze your own, unique path that will hopefully bring you happiness and fulfillment. This book is offered in the context of unconditional love.

Although this book is meant as a gift to you, it's your gift to me to watch you grow, develop, and mature.

That being said, let's jump in and explore.

SECTION 1:
THE BIGGEST DECISIONS

COLLEGE

Let's start with the big decision utmost on your mind, one that might feel the most relevant to you at this time. It's the first of many that will impact your success and happiness, although, in this instance, not as much as you would think.

As I write, you're wrapping up your college applications, a process that's exciting to watch. Of course, I hope you get into whichever colleges you want. As a biased parent, I think you deserve to get into every college to which you applied. The reality is many colleges are very selective and competitive. You will get into a college, but it might not be the one you desire most. Don't worry. It's extremely rare for college students to detest the institution they end up attending. It's such an amazing opportunity and experience that most people find themselves, eventually, happy. Of course, if you're truly unhappy at a college you can explore a transfer.

There are many colleges that will be a great fit and match for you. I think you could be happy at a big school, a small school, an urban school, or a rural school. The key to a successful experience is immersing yourself and devouring everything the school can offer.

Don't get impressed, enamored, or obsessed with the prestige and brand of any school. In the long run, it doesn't matter where you learn, but what you learn. The college experience is what it's about anyway.

You can go to an amazing school for four years and squander the opportunity, or you can go to a mediocre school and relish the experience. What you put into college and what you get out of it matters more than the brand or prestige.

I'll acknowledge that the more prestigious the school you attend, the more choices you will likely have post-graduation; but that attenuates over time based on many other factors.

Furthermore, remember that the goal of the game is to discover and pursue your own individual happiness.

So, embrace whichever college you land at, eschew the ranking or brand of the college, and just make the very most of the opportunity and experience you have. That will help you get the maximum from college and help propel you down a path of happiness and fulfillment.

College is an amazing experience. When we visited colleges together, I was jealous of the wonderful opportunity you'll have. College is a magical four-year period of your life that should be embraced, relished, and most of all, not wasted.

Although it might seem like being admitted to college is an ending point, particularly after all the hard work you did in high school and the daunting admission process, it's not an end—it's a new beginning. Enjoy the summer between your senior year of high school and your freshman year of college, but be ready to jump into college energetically, knowing you're starting over again in a new environment.

College is one of those moments in life when you realize everybody around you is excellent and talented; you've climbed up a layer in a pyramid. Perhaps in high school, you were amazing at math and a student leader and comfortable in your role as a senior. When you get to college, however, you'll soon realize everybody is fantastic at math and everybody was a student leader in high school, and now you're a modest freshman. Don't be intimidated. You'll find your spot: everybody does. But don't coast into college feeling too comfortable or entitled, because everybody earned admittance to your new college. It's a clean start and new beginning for an entire crop of kids, not just you.

As my friend Denise DeFiebre says, "At college, you can redefine yourself; it's a fresh beginning."

Just remember getting admitted to your dream college isn't the end of a chapter, it's your next starting line.

YOUR GOAL WHILE AT COLLEGE

The main goal of college is to learn how to learn; to become analytical, a critical thinker, and a great communicator. Most of all, it's to fully discover who you are and what you want in your life.

Go all in while at college. Don't coast through and do the least you can get away with. This is a narrow window in time where you can test and try different activities and experiences with few consequences. Try the hard English class; push yourself to give a new club sport a whirl; join the school newspaper.

Even if you're a rookie, this is the time to take it all in and expose yourself to experiences. Don't anchor yourself in easy and comfortable academic work. Go to the lecture, the performance, or the game. Participate in intramural sports and shows.

John Kenny, who has an undergraduate engineering degree, advocates a broad liberal arts undergraduate program that's not too career-centric. He believes this will best help a young adult develop the mind and creative thinking skills. The goal here is to get exposure and learn broadly. John specifically advocates studying and examining history and different religions, both of which are instructive and can help you learn and develop your own life philosophies.

It's hard to understand that the future chapters of your life will likely not have the freedom, flexibility, or the unlimited smorgasbord of resources and activities. So while in college, lean in—take full advantage.

THE PROBLEM WITH FREEDOM

Be careful during your first year of college. The shift from high school can be dramatic with newly found freedoms and the lack of imposed structure to your time.

You will witness kids who predominantly hang out and fritter away their time; they major in chillaxing. Obviously, you must have some down time, but in college, with little supervision and structure, you can easily slip into too much hanging out. This is a waste of time and expensive tuition dollars. Don't get caught in this trap.

Dennis Whittle, a Tar Heel from the University of North Carolina, echoes this sentiment. In our interview, he almost shouted, "Do not just hang out in college!" Explore, develop, test, discover, and be. But, hanging out in abundance is squandering an opportunity you will likely not have again in your lifetime. When you leave college, you'll regret not having plunged into the many opportunities presented.

GRADES

Geoff Dietzel told his son, Tom, "Don't mess around your first year. It is very hard to recover from poor grades. You should enjoy and grow, but remember your number one goal is academics. Absolutely ask for help if you need it."

Geoff and I shared a lot of time at college and I can assure you, we both could have spent far more time focused on academics. The transition from high school would have been far less jolting.

Many suggest grades do not matter as much as you might think. I'm not sure I fully agree. I think getting good grades in college does matter, but you shouldn't drive yourself crazy in the process. And while there's no big difference between an A and an A-, there is certainly a difference between an A- and a C.

The key: do your best. Worry about the input more than the outcome. You can control how much you study, with what regularity you study, and how much you apply yourself. I'm not sure you can fully control what the result will be.

If you get excellent grades in college, you'll have more choices after you graduate. However, I think I understand what people mean by saying grades don't matter as much as they thought: it's a nod towards enjoying and taking it all in, not missing meaningful opportunities and experiences at the expense of slightly better grades. I would not trade grades for too much hanging out, though.

Keep in mind, grades are a measure of studying and work, but don't necessarily reflect what you have learned and absorbed. College is an opportunity to broaden your horizons, so try not to fall into the rhythm of studying, memorizing, and regurgitating just to get a certain grade. You might think you have the system figured out, but you're just fooling yourself. It's worthwhile to study subjects, like philosophy, which train you to think for yourself and are specifically not about memorization.

GET INVOLVED

Marjorie Dorr's twenty-three-year-old son recently graduated from Boston College. Here's what he has to say: "Get involved. I did absolutely nothing with my time at BC, but luckily, I had good friend groups, and the culture at BC is great. However, my friends that were involved had way more fun, and an even larger friend group. Furthermore, companies (prospective employers) will ask you what you do in your spare time at college. It won't look good if you only can respond with 'Um, I drink and play video games/watch TV?'" His advice is pertinent, now that he's entered the real world.

MAKE INTERESTING, LIFELONG FRIENDS

While I encourage you to avoid hanging out too much, don't interpret this to mean you should not make new friends. The friendships you make in college can be lifelong and enduring. Invest in these friendships while in college and nurture and maintain them post-college. Sharing the college experience with peers will create strong bonds that are unique and special.

While there, you'll encounter people from all over the country and possibly all over the world. They will have different ideas and perspectives. Meet and befriend people in many social groups and expose yourself to their thoughts.

This is a great opportunity to interact with a group of talented and interesting people, to get their input. Try to meet a broad group and really learn who they are. These people, as well as their parents, can be models for you, allowing you to discover different paths you can take in your life.

DEVELOP THE 1.0 VERSION OF YOURSELF

When you finish college, you should have a fully formed sense of your values, goals, and identity. It doesn't matter what these are; there are no right or wrong answers—you simply need to find what works for you. This is really important and I encourage you to think about this in great detail while in college. And do so in writing, so it's real.

As Dennis Whittle suggests, college is a wonderful

place to develop the 1.0 version of yourself. After all, you're young and forming in college; who you become during this time is just the beginning. But the 1.0 version still matters, a lot. It will establish foundational elements of who you are and provide some guiding principles which will help you grow into your subsequent versions. It's very challenging to have a super 2.0, let alone a phenomenal 3.0, if the 1.0 is weak and riddled with flaws and emptiness.

GET TO KNOW YOUR ADVISORS

When in college, while you are fashioning and discovering this new you, get to know your professors and some administrators at school. These can be valuable mentors for you and help you navigate college life.

Typically, you'll be assigned an advisor upon arrival. Make it your business to regularly check in with your advisor and keep him or her plugged into your activities. Ask for advice and input. Advisors can often alert you to interesting opportunities and programs in school. You'll be amazed at what is out there just beyond your view.

WHAT TO STUDY

When thinking about what to study at college, pick something that interests you and fills you with passion. It might also be wise to contemplate how your studies ultimately will translate into a career. Again, your advisor can help with this. As I said, the main purpose of college is to learn how to learn, but you must also have some skills and a knowledge base that can help you find a job or be an entrepreneur. So, while I'm all for poetry, you might need to complement it with something more tangible, like physics, to help increase the probability of financial stability post college.

Do a bit of sleuthing; you'll find articles on which college majors earn what post college in the Suggested Reading section at the back of this book.

While I don't suggest you pick an academic major exclusively for vocational reasons, it should be part of your decision-making process.

VALUABLE EXTRACURRICULAR ACTIVITIES

Certain extracurricular activities in college can also propel you into a career. These are the kind of activities your advisor can point out. If you're interested in sports management, manage a team or be part of the Athletic Director's office. If you aspire to be in journalism, the school newspaper is calling you. Politics and public policy can be learned in the student government. Try to explore and test your interests with an eye towards what you might like to do after your college years.

STUDY ABROAD

While in college, you will likely have the opportunity to study abroad for a semester or year. This can be a wonderful experience and you should take advantage of the opportunity. It doesn't matter where, exactly, you study and visit, so much as doing it.

Living and studying abroad exposes you to new people, cultures, and languages. It gives insight into new models for living. It broadens your perspective and gives you a firsthand opportunity to understand different opinions and views. This makes you more mature and sensitive.

When I was in college, I was lucky to study in the then Soviet Union. You could not imagine a starker difference from life in the United States than being in the Soviet Union in 1987. It was (and literally felt like) a world away. It exposed me to a different government model and a different economic model; it introduced me to the people who inhabited the country. This was a fabulous, adventurous experience and a defining part of my college studies. My college advisor, Dick Sylvester, led the trip; I learned a great deal from him and value his friendship to this day.

The experience also made me grow up quickly. I had to learn to navigate the streets of Moscow and Leningrad independently, a satisfying challenge. Representing the American way of life while being peppered with questions from Russians made me feel like a deputized cultural ambassador.

After the official part of my study abroad experience, I traveled across the entire country (all nine time zones) on the Trans-Siberian Railway to the most eastern part of the Soviet Union. I did this with my intrepid friend, Doug Bruun, without the support of an official or organized program. We were literally out there on our own. It was great fun and an interesting way to see a country.

You, too, should see another country—to experience its people and culture first hand. I strongly encourage you to take advantage of this opportunity. Sometimes students pass on a study abroad experience because of a sport or not wanting to miss the social scene on campus. Get away. Create a lifelong memory. You will not regret it.

WHAT HAPPENS AFTER COLLEGE

When you finish college, you should be able to figure out how to get a job or start a business independently; how to manage your own finances; know where (and how) you'll live.

Mom and I, besides loving you unconditionally, will always provide you with advice (for whatever it's worth, and I'm wrong a lot), but we don't want to shower you with financial support or engineer a career for you by getting you a series of jobs. We really want you to make your own way and feel completely proud of what you accomplish and achieve. When parents are too engaged in helping their children, even if it comes from a loving place, they're creating children who are dependent rather than independent. We want you to struggle and flounder, and you surely will, but that very struggle is what will make you a stronger, more confident, and independent young adult. It's sort of like exercise a bit in that the struggle or challenge is actually what improves you and makes you stronger.

We want to foster independence and self-sufficiency. So, when you wrap up college, plan on being independent, but with unconditional love and all the free advice you want.

WRAP UP

Study for the sake of knowledge, not just good grades. Don't hang around too much. Take advantage of all the college experience has to offer. Make lifelong friends, bond with people from all walks of life, and form relationships with your advisor and professors, people who will make a point to nurture your development and identify good opportunities. The goal is to become independent, so you can enter the world knowing who you are and what you want.

DRUGS AND ALCOHOL

Many college students think of their undergraduate years as suspended reality, immune from laws and behavioral standards. This is just not true. College is not a protected bubble; wonderful things do happen, but so do harmful things. Drugs, drinking and driving, and rape will likely occur—do not have any part of it. Lives will change in an instant because of a brief lapse of judgment.

As a young adult, you are in a tenuous and wobbly part of your development. I know you have already witnessed drugs and alcohol in high school and have seen several students expelled for their poor choices and behavior. I am not going to be naïve and pretend that drugs and alcohol do not exist or that you will never have alcohol.

Drugs and alcohol are very destructive things, however, and you are most susceptible in your young adult years. At this stage, you're prone to seeking peer acceptance and approval; your values are not yet fully defined and internalized. This makes you vulnerable; and at-risk.

Drugs and alcohol can affect anybody. No one is immune

because of their upbringing, education, career, or the community in which they live. I have seen the devastating impact of addiction on the educated and uneducated, successful and unsuccessful alike. Your ethnicity does not matter, your background does not matter, and your religious orientation does not matter. Drugs and alcohol do not discriminate; they are equal opportunity predators. Expensive, status drugs are just as corrosive as cheap, street drugs. Sleekly branded alcohol supported by lavish marketing campaigns is equally as dangerous as low end, no frills booze.

If you are human, you are mentally and biologically at risk. Nobody is fully protected. We are all susceptible, regardless of who we are.

Unfortunately, you will have friends and acquaintances who derail their lives before they fully begin, due to drugs and alcohol. Don't let this be you.

RESPECT AND OBEY THE LAW

Before I expound on the dangers of these substances, let me emphasize the law. In Connecticut, for example, you're not allowed to have liquor until the age of twenty-one. I will not opine on the law, because there are many laws I do not agree with, but I respect and obey the law.

This is one of those rare instances where I will endeavor to set your course, weigh in heavily even though I encourage you elsewhere to make your own choice. As a family, we follow laws and I expect you to do so too. I know that sometimes people say that if you can serve in the military or vote, you should be able to consume alcohol.

But the law is the law. I encourage you to obey and follow all laws to the best of your ability, whether you agree with them or not.

DRUGS, SPECIFICALLY

Let me be unequivocal here. Drugs are illegal and unpredictable. Do not use them. People ingest drugs and don't know what they're putting into their bodies or where the substance came from. This is very dangerous and risky behavior and can cause all sorts of health problems.

There have even been drug problems in our family. My second cousin, Frank, is in his early forties and has bounced around from treatment programs, to jail, to shelters and has never quite gotten his life together. It's been hard for Frank to get or keep a job. You've heard about the challenges his addiction has caused him and the people who love him. Addiction is a disease that carries a heavy stigma in our society. Nobody knows whether the disease lies sleeping within, but it's your choice whether you tempt the disease by awaking it.

I know and recognize that addiction is a horrible disease, and I am not judging anybody who wrestles with it. I'm just trying to make you aware that bad choices, or very bad luck in being susceptible to addiction, can lead to very painful consequences.

"I always feared as a parent that my kids would turn to drugs, and once they hit that path, they had the potential to slide real deep," said Joe Smith, CEO of Connecticut-based Smith Brothers Insurance. "I have witnessed this, and it is tragic in that lives are wasted. The drain on family, friends, and society is so incredible. Some of this behavior is, of course, attributable to genetics or addictive personalities, but it also has to do with having a compass and having confidence or faith in living by your values. Day to day struggles or conflicts will come and go, so people cannot turn to destructive external help. You must get that help from within. It starts with self. You have to have self-esteem. There are other ways to manage stress, which cannot be avoided. So, how do you embrace it and manage it to be healthy? I think mindfulness and breathing techniques are simple daily techniques that can be done to help manage stress."

Because many people feel like Joe, I've included an entire chapter on religion and spirituality. For many people, this is a resource, an alternative to anesthetizing yourself during trying times and moments of self-doubt.

I'm not going to dwell on the risks and problems of illegal drugs because they're exactly that, illegal and you should not get involved with them in any way. The same can be said for prescription drugs used for unintended purposes.

THE PROBLEM WITH EXCESSIVE DRINKING

Excessive alcohol consumption is a problem in our country. There's nothing wrong with having a beer or two, or a glass of wine, with a meal. Truthfully, it can be enjoyable, even part of the culinary experience. What's unhealthy and very dangerous, however, is drinking to get drunk or drinking in excess—having six or twelve beers in two hours.

Having too much alcohol is dangerous to your health in many ways. You can experience alcohol poisoning, which can affect breathing and your heart rate and lead to death. You can drink and drive; an absolutely horrible choice. And you can say and do things while under the influence of alcohol that you'll regret.

In college, drinking will seem socially acceptable, the thing to do, but many of these people will leave school as full-blown addicts. Don't kid yourself; it could easily happen to you.

I certainly do not want to sound sanctimonious, because I drink beer and wine, although sparsely. And, when I was in college, I drank more.

When you get to college, drinking games will be part of

the landscape. Drinking for many becomes a sport. Just be aware—and be smart.

DRINKING UNTIL YOU BLACK OUT

Recently, I read a sobering (no pun intended) article in *The New York Times* by a senior at the University of North Carolina.[1] The article describes the college culture and practice of drinking to 'blackout'—where you lose all memory of an evening's events as well as total consciousness. The article describes drinking games and practices, which encourage drinking too much in short periods of time.

Ashton Katherine Carrick, the article's author, attributes this behavior to several factors.

First, college can be very stressful and intense. It is competitive and there is pressure to succeed. Drinking and blacking out are ways to escape and relieve pressure.

Second, it's cheap and easy to engage in this destructive behavior.

Third, the behavior is not looked down upon socially; rather, it's considered normal, even encouraged.

Carrick predominantly paints pressure as the driving catalyst of the behavior.

> "I think it's the stress. It permeates everything we do as college students. Many small, elite colleges are insanely competitive to get into in the first place and they remain competitive as students try to outdo one another with grades, scholarships, extracurricular activities and internships. Having been one of those hypercompetitive students, I can tell you that it never feels like enough. The person sitting next to you in class is always doing more and doing it better. I became obsessed with stacking my resume, even more so than when I was in high school. I saw it as a reflection of whether I would succeed in life. And I'm not alone. The obsession seems large-

ly driven by fear—fear of a crumbling job market, of not meeting parents' expectations, of crippling loan debt."

Try running, try meditation, or try watching a mindless movie on Netflix, but drinking with the intentional purpose of blacking out is dangerous and foolish.

Let's be clear: people die by doing this.

You need to be aware of the risks and consequences of making bad decisions around alcohol. And while a drink or two is likely OK, there's far more of a downside if you get too carried away.

ALCOHOL RELATED RISKS

Let me outline some immediate alcohol related risks associated with your age group.

Death: Each year, 1,825 students die from alcohol related injuries.[2] This strikes me as a huge number. If 1,825 people died from something else entirely, it would make for a headline news story. To further illuminate this risk, a risk not monopolized by students, the Centers for Disease Control (CDC) reports there are 88,000 deaths per year related to excessive alcohol in the United States.[3] Unfortunately, drinking deaths are isolated events that dribble out through the year, initiating little, if any, public reaction or outcry. Don't be a statistic: avoid risky behaviors.

Drunk Driving: Every year, particularly while you attend high school, then college, you'll hear about tragic things happening to young adults, and it almost always involves alcohol and cars.

According to the Center for Diseases Control (CDC), in 2014 alone, there were 9,967 alcohol related vehicular deaths.[4]

Life can change in an instant and mixing alcohol with cars is just a flat-out mistake. If you find yourself in a situation where you've had alcohol, or a friend has had alcohol, and no one is in any shape to drive, stop immediately. Get a taxi, get an Uber, get a hotel room. Do whatever you need to do, but do not get in a car with an impaired driver or attempt to drive impaired yourself. Call me. I don't care what time it is or where you are. I will not ask questions or judge. I will, instead, help by coming to get you or by getting transportation for you. Absolutely nothing can be worth the risk of driving with an impaired driver.

Date Rape: Unfortunately, alcohol fuels lots of bad behaviors. You will see that late nights and alcohol are perfect partners for trouble. Date rape (or any other classification of rape) is often related to the murky state of inebriation.

Jon Krakauer wrote an excellent book, *Missoula: Rape and the Justice System in a College Town*, which explores and details the role alcohol and drugs play in rape in college communities. According to Krakauer, alcohol and drugs are almost always present and abused when inappropriate sexual acts take place. Alcohol apparently emboldens people to make bad choices in this area.

Far fewer bad choices are made while sober at 2:00 p.m. than drunk at 2:00 a.m.

SETTING YOURSELF UP FOR ADDICTION

The problem with drugs and alcohol is that much of the damage they do can sneak up on you. It's not one isolated incident that takes you out at the knees, but the chronic buildup of a physical dependence, one equated with having a monkey on your back you cannot shed. Nobody sets out to be an alcoholic or drug addict; that cannot be possible. People drink or use drugs with a sense of invincibility; perhaps the alcohol and drugs amplify that sense of invincibility even more. Unfortunately, some people are at risk: they have the gene that sets them up for addiction. Nobody can be sure who is susceptible to addiction. The best way to avoid the risk is to avoid experimentation.

A few years ago, we saw former professional basketball player Chris Herren speak about drugs and alcohol. It was a powerful presentation that illustrated the life of an alcoholic and drug abuser, of an addict. It's hard to conceive that a person who achieved so much, who reached a lifelong dream of playing professional basketball, would risk it all by abusing drugs and alcohol, but he did. The picture he painted of a life in turmoil and disarray was heartbreaking.

You might recall in the Herren presentation that he felt the pull of addiction immediately when he first began experimenting with drugs and alcohol. There was no ramp up and no growing out of it phase. It was instantaneous.

I distinctly recall the chilling comment he made to the approximately 700 people in attendance. He said that 5 percent of you are addicts. You are either currently struggling with the disease, or will once you start to use alcohol or drugs. Herren went on to state that nobody knows in advance whether they are an addict or not. So the only sure way to be safe and avoid the risk is to not use drugs or alcohol at all.

There is a new drug awareness program called *Preventure* that identifies specific personality traits that make some adolescents more susceptible to drug and alcohol abuse than others. The program shows, in particular, that temperament can drive risk.[5]

Specifically, *Preventure* points out those adolescents with the following characteristics are at the highest risk:

- Sensation seeking

- Impulsiveness

- Anxiety sensitivity

- Hopelessness

You need to be aware of yourself and who you are. If you think you're at risk for biological reasons, addiction running in your family, or because of certain personality traits, you need to take such factors into account whenever you're exposed to addictive substances.

YOU'LL WISH YOU DID OTHER THINGS

Of course, when it comes to drinking to excess, not every loss seems so catastrophic, at least not on the surface. Live a little longer, however, and you'll realize that time spent wastefully, is time you can never get back.

At thirty-five, Jason Pananos' college memories are more recent than mine. When he was attending the University of Massachusetts at Amherst, he too drank excessively, and even abused alcohol. The rhythm at UMass, according to Jason, was to binge drink several times each week. Now, of course, he regrets all of the time he used partying and drinking in college, and during the few years thereafter. He used too much time socializing in a narrow way, where partying and alcohol were at the center, where recovering from the previous night's activities ate up an even larger chunk. He missed out on some college opportunities because he spent too much time going to parties and bars and missing out on other activities.

Jason shed that part of his life shortly after his college days and now lives close to UMass and periodically takes his wife and four children there to walk around and see the campus and college life. Jason notes, with amazement, that there is so much going on, and too much of it he missed. Now he wishes he spent more time running with friends and doing road races, and less time drinking.

Jason's experience is common and typical. I witnessed it myself at Colgate University, and participated in that lifestyle too. I feel similarly to Jason, in that college (and life) has so much to offer, so many things to experience. It's such a special opportunity, one you should take full advantage of and not squander by drinking dangerously and harming your body.

As you get older, you will likely not wish you went to drunken parties and instead took full advantage of college's resources.

SO, HOW DO YOU AVOID THIS?

One way to avoid drugs and excessive alcohol use is to side-step those who embrace that lifestyle. At times this will be awkward, even painful, as it may result in broken friendships. Peer pressure can be very powerful and intimidating. I totally get and understand this and have been subject to it myself. But, if you surround yourself with friends and people who want similar things to you, and make healthy life choices, you are less likely to be in risky, pressure-inducing situations.

Willy MacMullen, the headmaster of the Taft School, agrees that, particularly during adolescence, you need to think about whom you surround yourself with as friends and allies—especially in the area of drugs and alcohol. Do you have friends who have your well-being at heart? Are they helping you and looking out for you? Are you helping them and looking out for them?

The Gordie Foundation is a nonprofit organization which was founded to honor the senseless and unnecessary death of an eighteen-year-old freshman at the University of Colorado in 2004. The Foundation focuses on providing today's young people with the skills to navigate the dangers of alcohol, binge drinking, peer pressure, and hazing. It is also a cautionary tale about surrounding yourself with people who have your back.

Gordie Bailey had a lot going for him. Hailing from Deerfield Academy, he had been a football captain and lacrosse player involved in music and drama. He had been at Colorado for all of one month when he attended a pledging event for prospective fraternity members. There, he was required to consume a certain amount of alcohol in a very short period of time. Having passed out, he was placed on a couch to sleep it off. He never woke up.

I can't imagine that the people who encouraged Gordie to drink too much alcohol, then did not help him when he obviously needed help the most, were really his true friends. If that is the definition of a friend, you can live without them. I can't fathom being Gordie, or the fraternity members who catalyzed the behavior, or Gordie's parents, or anybody else involved in this awful scene.

Unfortunately, these things absolutely do happen. Do not be near anything that remotely looks or feels like this. Pick your friends and allies carefully because as Willy suggests, your life might depend on it.

I've never interacted with a businessperson, family member, or friend and said to myself, "Wow, he's a great guy. I like and admire him because he drinks excessively, or does drugs." As a matter of fact, when I see people behave like that, I feel awkward, and it seems odd to me. Even now, at my age, I see people who place alcohol at the center of their social life. They literally cannot be in a social situation without alcohol.

YOUR INTERNAL COMPASS

When I had too much alcohol in college, it really stemmed from my own social insecurities and a lack of personal core. I had not yet fully determined how I wanted to behave and I made choices I would not make today. I periodically succumbed to social pressures and that was just weakness on my part.

I hope you have more self-confidence and awareness than I did.

Ted Heavenrich, a teacher from Taft, told me about his experience with drugs when he attended Oberlin College in the seventies. When his parents dropped him off at school, the dorm halls stunk of marijuana. You could cut the haze as you walked down the hall. Ted felt like 95 percent of the school used marijuana back then, and he was goaded into joining in. Yet, Ted did not want to be part of that environment and politely rejected his friends' attempts to get him to be a marijuana smoker.

On one occasion, someone left a joint underneath his dorm room door in an envelope. Ted was offended and marched into the room of the suspected perpetrator and announced that he absolutely did not want it, that it was his choice whether to be part of that scene, or not, and that he did not appreciate the constant pressure.

Ted displayed a lot of self-awareness and fortitude by rejecting the persistent barrage of pressure. Ted attributes this to his ability to be true to himself, to knowing what he wanted. He also discovered that you must be careful about who you surround yourself with because their behaviors will influence yours.

Recently, I was at a dinner with a group of friends. It was a warm environment with nice conversation. Everybody was drinking wine, except for me. I was just not really in the mood for wine and I had a long drive home at the end of the evening. I politely demurred when offered a drink, but my friends kept insisting that I have some with our dinner. I kept rebuffing the offers, awkwardly. The dinner reminded me of my conversation with Ted, and that the pressure and behaviors Ted observed in his twenties persist today.

What I found funny about that dinner, was the fact that I see this group of friends a handful of times each year and I truly enjoy their company and conversation. But it seems odd to me that they actually care about what I eat or drink. I successfully manage to ingest food and beverages the 360 days each year I do not see them, so why would I need their intervention now?

So you see, even when you reach my age, people will want you to engage in behaviors that might not be your choice. I did not have wine that evening; and although I do cherish those friendships, I'm OK with the relationships changing if I choose not to do something just to fit in.

As Ted said, be true to yourself.

WRAP UP

If you choose to drink when it's legal for you to do so, drink sparingly. Be in control. Pray you don't have a gene that makes you susceptible to addiction.

Often people will drink excessively because they lack self-confidence and awareness and are actually seeking to conform and belong. Don't seek approval from your peers by drinking excessively; this is flat out stupid. I know that in my introduction I promised not to be prescriptive, but on this topic I will diverge and tell you explicitly: do not drink excessively. It's dangerous. If you feel pressure to drink from your friends or peers, they're the wrong ones. Don't care what they think on this topic. Have your own security and self-confidence to resist the pressure to drink abusively. You will be far happier in the long run.

And just to reiterate: Drugs are illegal and just not something to do.

HEALTH

Since we're on the topic of eschewing substances that will compromise your well-being, let's talk about health. Health and a high-performing body are truly treasures and the greatest gifts and forms of wealth. No matter what you have materially or achieve in your life, it will not matter at all without the benefit of health.

Good health can be tenuous and you should do everything possible to tilt the odds in your favor, but realize that even if you do everything right, you can still draw an unlucky card.

At seventeen you are fit, strong, and physically invincible. It's a wonderful feeling. When we ski, bike, or run together, I ache the next day and you have no apparent recovery challenges at all. I'm jealous. As hard as it for you to imagine, one day you will moan, as I do, "Oh, my back!"

Health is one of those things in life that's far easier to maintain than fight to recover. So, let's talk about how to do just that.

ESTABLISH HEALTHY HABITS

As you enter your twenties, you're establishing lifelong health habits that will determine whether you are a participant or a spectator in your forties and fifties. These habits are all about choice.

Consider these sobering statistics:

- Currently, more than one third of the adult U.S. population is defined as obese.[6]

- Heart disease is the number one cause of U.S. deaths at 614,348 of 2.6 million deaths (23 percent).[7]

- Currently, 16.8 percent of U.S. adults are smokers and this is the leading cause of preventable deaths in the U.S.[8]

- Almost 24 percent of U.S. adults get zero leisure time physical activity.[9]

This does not paint an attractive picture for health in our country. I should note, some trends are certainly improving, so the data is not all bleak.

What are some guidelines to help your health?

- **Do not smoke—ever.** This vile, expensive, and highly addictive habit is totally avoidable. 68 percent of U.S. adult smokers want to quit. Why would you ever start something that the vast majority of participants want to stop? Sadly, smokers who actually have stopped smoking represent a small 6.2 percent.[10] So, most smokers want to stop and relatively few are able to do so. That's bad math. Never, never smoke.

- **When in a car, wear a seat belt.** Motor vehicle accidents are the single leading cause of death in fifteen to twenty-four year-olds in the U.S. Furthermore, using a seatbelt reduces injury and death rates by half. When driving, insist all people in the car wear a seatbelt and absolutely make sure you do.[11]

- **Nutrition will, to a large extent, determine your health.** A quick online book retailer search returns 119,115 books on nutrition. Since there are many conflicting philosophies and ideas around the subject, I'll simply share a few generally accepted thoughts:

  ◄ **You cannot eat enough fruits and vegetables**. This should be a large portion of your daily diet. Try to have at least some fruit and vegetable intake at every meal, even breakfast. Fruits and vegetables contain fiber, which fills you up; and nutrients, which are good for your body. Fruits and vegetables have carbohydrates, a source of energy. These carbs are complex and beneficial as compared to simple carbohydrates, such as white bread.

  ◄ **Unprocessed food is better than processed food**. Food that is as close to nature as possible has fewer chemicals and is therefore better for you. Try to eat things that are fresh, or foods you have prepared, instead of canned, boxed, or defrosted.

  ◄ **Some sweets and sugary foods are OK**. When it comes to sweets, a little goes a long way. Be reasonable. Try to avoid excessive candy, cookies, and ice cream.

  ◄ **Try to eat more fish than chicken or red meat**. These are sources of protein and are important for you. Red meat tends to have more fat and cholesterol than chicken and fish, so too much can create problems. Focus on fish.

  ◄ **Whole grains are good for you—they're also filling**. Simple grains, like rice and wheat, are not good carbohydrates. When choosing breads or cereals, try to go with complex carbs instead of simple carbs.

- **Exercise**. The truth is, you really don't need to do that much of it to enjoy a positive impact.[12] More is better and can just be fun, especially if your exercise is in the form of games or activities you enjoy. Make exercise a way to interact with friends and do it on a regular basis.

- **Socialize**. Many studies have documented that vibrant social interactions are not only fun, but good for you. Build close friendships and maintain family relationships as part of a well-balanced health program.

- **Sleep**. Get an adequate amount of sleep to recharge your mind and body.[13] Required hours of sleep will differ by person, but generally shoot for seven to nine hours of sleep. All-nighters are painful and difficult to recover from the next day. You cannot catch up on sleep deprivation by sleep binging on weekends. Try to have regular, consistent sleep patterns for the best health.

- **Be an attentive driver.** Distracted driving is prevalent amongst young adults, especially in the age of cell phones. Taking your eyes off the road while traveling at 50 mph is the same as closing your eyes. Please, please do not text while driving. Nothing is so important that it can't wait. If you truly need to text, pull over. According to a federal study, distracted driving causes 16 percent of vehicle fatalities per year.[14] Do not risk your life, or the life of anyone else, with this foolish behavior. Your world can literally change in one second.

- **Be optimistic**. Having a sunny outlook and disposition will help you live longer and have fewer
illnesses according to Harvard Medical School.[15]
In the words of Joe Smith, "I think it is very important to look at the positives in any situation. It
not only allows you to not be biased or shaped by
daily events that may be negative, but it also brings
you happiness. Ultimately, you're more effective
and influential as a leader and friend."

Keep everything in moderation. I'm not suggesting you
embrace an ascetic lifestyle, but be conscious about excessive-
ness that can be deleterious to your long-term health.

SELF-INFLICTED WOUNDS VS. THE UNLUCKY CARD

As you can see, many choices you make can greatly support
your health. On the flip-side, there are choices you make
that will undermine your ability to live a long and vital life.
Self-inflicted wounds, I call them; they're health choices you
make that are known to increase negative outcomes.

A simple example: smoking. Irrefutable and overwhelming data prove smoking decreases life expectancy by increasing
the likelihood of certain types of cancers and disease. Nobody
forces you to smoke. It's not a bad card you are dealt. So, if
you choose to smoke and it causes lung cancer, for example,
that's a self-inflicted wound.

Knowing what we know, why would anyone make this
choice? It's tantamount to placing a gun to your head and
playing Russian roulette.

It's important to differentiate between a self-inflicted
wound and drawing an unlucky card. A person can do everything right with nutrition, exercise, avoiding excessive
alcohol and abstaining from tobacco, and still get a bad card
in the form of a disease or illness. This is just the randomness

of life and cannot be avoided.

However, it's ridiculous to claim, after ignoring blatant evidence, that self-destructive behavior and its consequences are the same as bad luck.

You will unquestionably encounter people who embrace the philosophy of living for the moment and indulging in excessive food, alcohol, or tobacco. This person will often say silly things like, "You don't know when your number is up," or "What doesn't kill you will make you stronger." You may even hear, "Live hard, die young, and leave a good looking corpse." That's ridiculous.

I, for one, would like to live to a ripe old age, disease-free.

TAKING IT FOR GRANTED

Health is fragile and tenuous. When you're in good health you feel invincible, full of vigor and confidence. You assume you will be able to do the things you now enjoy, forever. When your health is compromised, however, you quickly realize that good health is precious—and why it's so very important to make the most of it.

That's something Rachel Albert wishes she would have known when she was younger. Maybe then she would have created some lifetime experiences, such as visiting Africa or climbing Machu Picchu, while she could have, before rheumatoid arthritis limited certain activities.

Life is precious, just ask Rick Richardson. Two of Rick's three daughters have faced serious health events. These not only scared the family, but led to multiple hospital stays, changes in lifestyle, and doctors galore. Rick personally understands the dear gift of health and he now views the two daughters who encountered health issues differently. He appreciates the fragility of it all.

For Eric Wisnefsky, it was his family background that influenced his healthy habits. His sister was diagnosed with diabetes as a young child. Because of this, Eric was exposed to a nutritionist and began to understand the benefit of healthy eating habits. When Eric and his wife, Tammy, had children, they made a conscious decision to make health a priority and a central part of their lives. Eric exercises regularly and, with Tammy, adheres to healthy eating habits. Tammy meticulously plans weekly menus for their busy family. This helps them stick to healthy choices and keep the necessary food in the house to build healthy meals and make good decisions.

Your health can change in an instant. Your objective should be to do everything within your control to increase the probability of remaining healthy.

WRAP UP

I hope you plan on living to 100, and I hope you plan on being active the entire journey. Taking care of your health will not only increase the probability of extending your life, it will also enhance the quality of your life. Hike in your nineties, ski in your eighties. Be the oldest entrant at the 5k race. Live well knowing it can all be taken away by fate, or sheer carelessness.

DATING, SEX, AND WHOM YOU MARRY

Once you enter your young adult years, your twenties, you will likely, at some point, meet your future spouse—maybe even in college. Whom you marry is probably the single most important decision you will make, one that stands to affect your well-being and happiness.

But before we talk about marriage, we must address the prerequisite: dating and sex. Awkward, yes, but really important. In these arenas, a lot of mistakes get made.

I'm not going to pretend I am an expert on dating, since I've not done it in about 28 years. Also, I do not pretend to know how experienced you are in the whole relationship department, so allow me to paint an overview of how they tend to develop, then deepen.

While in college (as in high school), you'll be friends with girls, which is fantastic and healthy. These platonic friendships will give you the opportunity to understand and appreciate girls as equals and peers. You will learn a lot from these pals, which will help when you enter into romantic relationships.

Of course, many young people 'hook up,' or have some type of sexual interaction without necessarily dating or being a couple. When you do this, just be respectful and aware of the nature of your relationship and the expectations this arrangement entails. This leads me to the first topic . . .

HOW TO TREAT WOMEN

First, you must be respectful to women. You do not have to fall in love with every girl you date or 'hook up' with, but you must be polite, respectful, and understand all limitations. You should never say anything bad about a girl you dated to your friends or on social media. That is totally inappropriate. What you share with a girl is private and not for gossiping, especially on social media.

Try to think of it this way: one day I hope you have a daughter. How would you want people to treat your daughter?

When you are intimate with a woman, you must absolutely respect all of her boundaries and wishes. Failing to do so could not only hurt one or both of you, it may also lead to severe legal consequences. It is considered rape if you have certain sexual interactions with a woman without her consent. You should be very clear with a woman as you proceed sexually to absolutely confirm that what you are doing is consensual. I know this might sound awkward and unromantic, but it is extraordinarily serious.

Now, I don't want to imply that you should not engage in certain activities exclusively because of the consequences. That is not true. You should never push a woman sexually because it's flat-out wrong. Additionally, if you do push a woman sexually, there are life altering consequences which will fall entirely on your shoulders. These consequences can include prison and becoming a registered sex offender—a label that will never go away.

AVOID DANGEROUS SITUATIONS

In 2015, Owen Labrie, a student at St. Paul's, an elite prep school in Concord, New Hampshire, was convicted of sexual assault. He received a one-year prison sentence; and became a registered sex offender for life. Labrie was only twenty years old at the time. I have to assume he did not set out to assault or rape a fellow student; rather, it was a series of events gone wrong. This tragic incident changed the victim's life, the offender's life, and the lives of their respective families. Do not do this to another person or yourself. Do not be in a situation where you can remotely be assailed for inappropriate or illegal behavior: it can be devastating for too many people.

It bears repeating: the best way to stay fully clear of this type of situation is to make sure that anytime you are with a woman you are getting explicit and clear verbal signals that all activities are OK. If a woman is drunk or has taken drugs, she is likely unable to affirmatively consent to sexual activity and you should steer clear of that situation. If a woman is drunk or using drugs, you should help her to a safe place and get medical attention, if necessary.

Rape is a growing problem on college campuses. You will likely see painful situations and disrespectful behavior. Do not be that person who causes them. It is bad form and you will not like yourself for being anywhere near that.

USE BIRTH CONTROL

When you do have sex with a woman, it's extremely important to use birth control every single time. Use birth control to protect yourself from sexually transmitted diseases and from unintentional conception. Do not believe any nonsense about one time, or time of the month, or withdrawal: use protection. All concerns of pregnancy aside, you must use a condom unless you are absolutely certain you are not at risk of sexually transmitted diseases. Do not make a foolish mistake that can change your life.

Children are fantastic (I'm blessed with three wonderful

children), but you need to be emotionally ready for kids; you need to have the financial resources to raise those kids. Having a child too early, with the wrong person, or when you are not ready can unintentionally change your life course. You cannot be prepared for a child until you have made the contemplative and emotional decision to go down that path.

THE MOMENTUM CURVE

The dangers of sex aside, there's another natural byproduct of intimacy that you should be aware of. Somewhere in your twenties or early thirties, you will likely begin to think about marriage. There may even be forces that push you in that direction. Everybody around you will start to get engaged, and then married; before long, you'll be on a momentum curve that moves you along, as if by magic, from dating right into marriage.

Here is how it happens: first you start dating; you meet each other's friends; then you meet the family; you start traveling together; pretty soon, people are asking when you're going to get married; you get engaged; and boom, you're married.

Marriage is awesome if you have the right partner. It can be very painful and difficult if you do not have the right partner. That's why the momentum curve is worth mentioning and being aware of.

WHOM YOU MARRY

I am extraordinarily lucky. I've been married to Mom for twenty-four years—and would marry her again in a second (I hope she feels the same). I hope you have a wife who is just as fantastic, whom you love as much as I love her. So when it comes to whom you should marry, make the decision as if it is monumental and has enormous consequences, because it is, and it does. You cannot depend on luck alone.

Luck does play a significant role in marriage, however. If you are fortunate and enjoy good health, happy children without significant challenges, and stable finances, there is a higher probability your marriage will succeed. If some of these factors are not present, there will be more stress in the marriage, and that can be riskier.

No doubt that's why most people I interviewed would bestow the "magic card" upon their children in hopes they'd use it in choosing the right marriage partner. People responded this way regardless of their situation; whether they had experienced divorce or were in a healthy marriage.

What's interesting about this issue is I was never once educated on how to find the right person to marry, or how to build a terrific marriage once married. There were no courses in high school, college, or graduate school. Mentors, loving parents, friends, and coaches—nobody ever pulled me aside and shared with me the enormity of this decision. Nobody pointed out the things I should be thinking about when approaching this decision. Nothing, zero input.

That's crazy, because 40 to 50 percent[16] of marriages in the U.S. today end in divorce. Divorce is a very messy and ugly separation process that hurts families and enriches lawyers. I would not want to go through a divorce, and hope you don't either. My friends who have unfortunately experienced divorce describe it as painful emotional carnage where nobody wins.

How do you prevent a divorce? Have the right spouse. How do you have the right spouse? Well, that is a very important question, one I intend to answer as best I can.

THE BASIS FOR A SUCCESSFUL MARRIAGE

Sometimes people begin a relationship based on physical attraction. I'm not saying this is wrong, but it might not be enough to serve as a strong foundation for a lifelong partnership. People age; looks change or fade with time. If physical attributes were too large a part of why you chose a spouse, you might be on a bad path. In the words of Jason Pananos, "Love is not attraction. Love is purely something you do for someone else."

Successful marriages are based on character and compatibility. You need to be with someone who shares the same life philosophies, principles, and values. It is, therefore, important to know your own life philosophies, principles, and values, before you can match with those of another. I'm not suggesting you need to be identical with your spouse, but a material overlap is important.

THE AGE THING

Part of making a good match involves knowing who you are and where you are in your life cycle. I got married when I was twenty-seven and I think it was slightly on the young side. I would suggest you think about thirty as a moment when you might be emotionally ready to get married.

I'm not alone in advocating that you hold off on this decision. Marjorie Dorr, former CEO of Anthem Blue Cross in Connecticut, got married to her husband when she was twenty-three. She has a fantastic marriage but according to her, she's lucky it worked. That's why she encourages her two sons to wait until they are at least thirty to get married. "You are still figuring out who you are in your twenties, and you do not need any additional constraints. Your twenties are an opportunity to develop a firmer understanding of who you are."

Your job in college and during your twenties is to establish yourself as a person and fully move into young adulthood. You must figure out your life philosophies, values, principles and goals. Until you have these firmly established, you cannot know what you want and need in your life. Anecdotally, my friends who married on the young side seem to have had higher divorce rates than those who married a bit later. This is certainly not statistical evidence, just observational (and I do know many people who married on the young side and have healthy, happy marriages). Furthermore, friends I know who have divorced and remarried are much clearer and explicit about what they want in a second marriage, because they have experience and wisdom.

Case in point: Sarah Bowen Shea, author of *Run Like a Mother*, married her first husband in her early twenties; he was her college sweetheart. Looking back, she realizes she wasn't ready to be married. She was still figuring out who she was. She also admits that having another person in your life in your early twenties, when there's so much to explore in your own life and in the world around you, can complicate, or limit, that exploration and can be burdensome. So, while marrying young can be the right answer for some people, if you're thinking about it, you should absolutely take a break before taking that step.

Waiting is a good idea, even if you can make it work. It'll give you the ability to develop as an individual.

My mom (Grandma Linda to you) married when she was twenty. It's hard for me to imagine—as I write, you're eighteen; the thought of you being married in two years seems unfathomable. But it was quite common in her era. My mom said she was totally unprepared to be married at that age. She didn't have the life skills or maturity to take that step, even though she's been married to my dad for fifty-four years.

Because she married so young, my mom was never alone or independent. She made note of this: she went from living at home and attending college locally at Brooklyn College—for *eight dollars* per semester—to getting married. In such circumstances, it's hard to develop a sense of self. That's why she advocates waiting to marry: so you can explore, grow, and test things out for yourself.

THE SOUL MATE THING

One of the reasons people marry so young, particularly college sweethearts, is the fear that they will never find another person they will love as much. It's the fear of missing out. As much as I love your mom, I think there are multiple people who you can marry and be happy with. I say this because you should not be in a rush to get too serious with somebody too soon. As a young adult, you should date enough people to understand what works for you and what works for a potential partner. You should explore and discover different types of relationships and understand who you are before getting too entwined too early. There is not one single soul mate for you; there are many potential soul mates. The trick is to find the right one when you are both intellectually, chronologically, and emotionally ready to make a lifelong commitment together.

Being a young adult is the time to experience lots of different things, in many parts of your life; it's a time to discover who you are and what you want your life to be. I'm not suggesting you be selfish or self-centered; but take your time committing to a serious relationship, so you have the chance to get to know yourself, without the burden of responsibilities.

In other words, don't be scared of missing "the one;" live and explore, and when you're ready, there will be a right one.

KNOW WHAT YOU'RE SIGNING UP FOR

Who is the right one for you? That's the question. Many

people shared with me that they believe marriage is easier and has a higher probability of success if the two partners are substantially similar. This helps the marriage have a common starting point and understanding of perspective. If the marriage participants have vastly different backgrounds, it might be more difficult for the partners to understand each other. When challenges occur, and they will, it might exacerbate the differences and create difficulties.

I'm not proposing, at all, that dissimilar people with varied backgrounds cannot have a successful marriage. I'm only encouraging you to think deeply about compatibility and shared perspective and a sense of alignment. All of these things will help make for a better partnership and increase the likelihood of success.

I don't know if opposites attract or whether people with a high degree of similarity will do better in marriages. What I do know is that you need to be perfectly lucid on what you are signing up for. Different is OK as long as you know how you will interact; the same is OK as long as you know how you will interact. There needs to be a clear understanding of what the two parties want and need in order to make the marriage successful. Of course, one spouse might enjoy tennis while the other favors cycling—that's wonderful to share diverse interests and hobbies, or even have separate interests and hobbies. But, the moral compasses of each party need to be properly calibrated to make it work.

TOPICS TO THINK ABOUT BEFORE MARRIAGE

Here's what I mean by calibration: certain philosophical issues and preferences need to be determined, agreed upon before you commit to spending the rest of your life with someone. **Before** being the key word. These are the issues known to be deal breakers if there is not agreement:

- Where do you want to live and why?

- How important is extended family and what do you think relationships will be with extended family?

- How important is money and why?

- Will you be spenders or savers?

- What will you spend money on and why?

- What role will religion play and can you integrate and share religious backgrounds and values?

- How many children do you want to have and when?

- How will childcare work?

- How will education work?

- Will you do all, some, or none of your hobbies and activities together?

- How do you feel about politics; and can you respect each other's views if they are different?

- How will both of your careers work in the marriage?

- Will both of you work, or not?

- Are both careers equally important in the marriage?

- What traditions and rituals will you bring into the marriage from each background?

- What are your communication styles? Do you calmly talk things out or scream and fight? Do you hold grudges or move on quickly?

- How will you resolve conflicts (which are inevitable)?

- Do you make each other smile and laugh?

You can find more on this in the Suggested Reading section, at the back of the book.

I know it doesn't sound very romantic to think about or discuss these topics while dating or as you approach marriage. But, these are the very topics that cause conflict in marriages. You don't necessarily need to agree on every topic, but you should at least be aware of what you are signing up for, so you can make a conscious choice about whether this is a good match, or not.

Will Thorndike, an experienced and successful businessperson, takes it a bit further by speaking of marriage in common business vocabulary. Specifically, he encourages as much diligence as possible. In a business setting, diligence is defined as research and analysis of a company or organization done in preparation for a business transaction; practically, this translates into dating for a long time, seeing how you and your potential partner interact in different settings and situations, attempting to have meaningful, philosophical conversations to explore compatibility on higher levels, spending a lot of time with each other's families.

Marriage, by the way, is a coming together of more than two individuals. In other words, in-laws matter (luckily, I have delightful in-laws). Not only will you have to interact with them on a regular basis, looking at their relationships may also provide a glimpse into your future. After all, we sometimes fall back into the patterns our parents modeled for us. Such patterns will often be evident.

TAKE A TEST DRIVE

One of the best ways of getting to know a potential mate, besides looking at her family dynamics, is to live with her. Mom and I lived together for just over a year prior to getting engaged and married. Not only was it great fun, it also confirmed for me that I was incredibly fortunate and wanted to spend my life with her.

"Take a test drive," that's what Marjorie Dorr suggests. Although it wasn't a tenable choice when she was in her early twenties, with her Midwest upbringing and all, Marjorie fully believes you should live together before you get married. It's a full on simulation of marriage, with low switching costs, and little, if any social stigma (for most people).

Living together prior to marriage used to be considered socially taboo; that's certainly not the case now. I think it's something you should absolutely do.

FRIENDSHIP FIRST, MARRIAGE SECOND

Dave Schnadig and his wife, Lori, were friends before they began dating. This gave them a different perspective on who they were as people, allowing them to make a more objective decision on their relationship and fit as life partners.

Dave points out that when thinking about marriage, you should try to make a rational decision in the context of a very emotional decision-making process. Knowing each other first as friends helps.

You see, when you experience love, your thought processes and emotions swirl about. Engaged in a form of infatuation, you're not really in the best place to make a very important life decision. You need to pause, as hard as that is, and make sure you actively think through the decision in as rational way as possible, despite the whirlwind. Dave sees marriage as a seminal event in your life, one you should approach with patience and a clear head. Starting with friendship and respect can help ensure you'll have a strong partnership, even if the passion cools.

YOU COMPLETE ME

Romantics tend to believe they cannot be whole without the object of their affections. Even if you don't consider yourself a romantic, the tumultuous emotions that accompany love can make you believe the very same thing.

Here's Marjorie's take: "I am already complete, and my husband makes me better. I do not need Len; I want Len." In other words, to be in a successful marriage, you need to stand on your own and not be dependent on your partner in an unhealthy way. Marjorie and Len, married for thirty years, consider themselves to be low-maintenance and independent, and that helps make their marriage successful.

So, keep in mind: you may be better together; but you're complete on your own.

KEY ATTRIBUTES FOR A SUCCESSFUL PARTNERSHIP

There are certain hallmarks of a relationship that make for a long and successful union. Judy Bernstein, my cousin and a psychologist, shares some of these key attributes here. They include:

- Mutual respect being important to both people
- Having similar core values
- Having some similar interests
- The capacity to remember kindness in all interactions—no cruelty
- The ability to be yourself with your partner, not a contrived version
- Honest communication
- The ability to navigate and negotiate when there is a problem
- The ability to deal with stress, the avoidance of the type that makes a person not present in the relationship
- Being fully present and paying attention when the other person is talking

If there's alignment on these topics, and others, you're beginning the partnership moving in the same direction.

These attributes alone will not guarantee success, but they do increase the probability.

ONE SIZE DOES NOT FIT ALL

With all of the common issues that need to be considered, the attributes that need to be nurtured and developed, it may seem that there are way too many boxes that need to be checked before you commit to another, so why bother?

Sarah Bowen Shea offers there can be many forms of marriage that can be successful for different couples. Marriage is not a one-size-fits-all concept. According to her, your partner need not tick every box, and will likely not be able to do so. Even if you were able to find someone who represents an exact match at a given point in time, people change as they mature. Not only do people evolve, marriages can contract and expand over time as well. At some moments, your lives may feel very intense and intertwined, and at others, they may feel like a train track that is connected and moving in the same direction yet with two separate rails.

GROW TOGETHER

Let me highlight the word growth for a minute. In your long-term partnership—spanning decades—you and your spouse will evolve and change. You have to. Part of the fun of marriage is growing together and influencing each other's development as a person and, in combination, the marriage. You cannot go into a multi-decade relationship expecting a static status. You have to embrace the change and growth because it's inevitable. If both partners are committed to accepting change and working together to make that change positive, while giving more than half the effort to the relationship, there is a good chance the marriage will stay on a fantastic track.

DATE YOUR WIFE

If people change, if marriages contract and expand over time, how do you make your relationship rock solid? Keep dating your wife. Marriage is not an end, it's a beginning and to make it successful you need to be attentive, invested, and emotionally engaged, just like when you were dating.

Typically, people are on their best behavior when dating. They're focused and polite; they plan fun activities and are generally interested in the other person. Once married, it may be easy to forget that dating behavior and slip into some bad habits, which lead to friction.

But, as Bob Zelinger reminds us, "Marriage needs feeding and watering. You must put into it for it to be healthy. You cannot expect to only take out of it."

Most of my friends who talk about their failed marriages note a common theme of losing a connection due to the inevitable demands and activity of life. Marriage can easily slip into feeling like coworkers and just trying to hold it all together. That does not have to be the case at all and can be combated by carving out time together with your spouse to do things as a couple. Marriage absolutely becomes a lot harder when kids come into the picture. But for a marriage to work, sustain and thrive, you need to remember why you got married in the first place.

Many people have a date night; they bike, run, or watch movies together. The specific activity is irrelevant as long as you share some meaningful time together where the energy and focus are on each other and not on something else.

Sometimes a married couple is actually a pair of married single people. Their busy lives prevent them from fully being a team that operates together. You do not want this.

ME TIME

Equally important to a healthy marriage, is having some independent time and space, either by yourself or with friends. Finding the right mix is important. I have always felt that when I do things on my own, I have the opportunity to bring something back to the marriage. If you experience absolutely everything together, there's no need to bring back unique ideas to share with each other.

FEED THE RIGHT WOLF

My friend and mentor, Tom Bird, recently shared a story with me about how to build a successful marriage. I would like to share it with you . . .

When asked to speak at a friend's wedding, he shared this Native American parable:

> A grandfather is talking with his grandson and he says there are two wolves inside each of us, which are always at war.
>
> One of them is a good wolf, which represents things like kindness, bravery, and love. The other is a bad wolf, which represents things like greed, hatred, and fear.
>
> The grandson stops and thinks about it for a second then he looks up at his grandfather and says, "Grandfather, which one wins?"
>
> The grandfather quietly replies, "The one you feed."

When discussing this story with Tom and how it relates to marriage, Tom pointed out that we all have both wolves inside of us: one, which basically represents the good, and one, which represents the bad. In a marriage, if we always find fault and disappointment with our spouse or our situation, we are feeding the bad wolf. If we look for the positive and good in our spouse, we are feeding the good wolf.

The parable clearly points out that whichever wolf you feed will prevail. This is an active choice, not a set of cards you are randomly dealt. Do not kid yourself. If you embrace and feed the good wolf within you, it's more likely your marriage will grow, develop, and thrive. You have much more control than you might think.

AFTER THE CRASH

As a divorce attorney, Rick Richardson has something of a backstage pass to a lot of marriages that didn't work. While he doesn't see the marriages begin to disintegrate, nor does he have full visibility on why they're dissolving, he is the first person there after the crash.

So I asked him why, from his vantage point, so many marriages in our society don't work and what he would share with his three daughters to make their marriages more successful.

The first habit Rick attributes to failed marriages: people just don't work on them actively; they take the marriage for granted. Rick drew the analogy to a business: you cannot expect a business to grow and thrive and evolve without constant attention, thought, and constructive examination. Marriages behave the same way. Too often, when he speaks to a person seeking a divorce, the reason their marriage fell apart is they basically stopped participating. Of course, marriages end for a myriad of reasons—including infidelity and addiction issues—but the vast majority, according to Rick, melt from malaise.

To counter this, Rick suggests spouses immediately address and discuss anything that is not on track in the marriage and prevent it from festering and compounding over time. Rick proposes immediate, direct, and honest communication can mitigate a lot of the problems that can develop in marriage. Rick noted that if one partner thinks there's a problem in the marriage, there's a problem in the marriage. There need not be consensus. If one party feels negative about the relationship, there will be an impact on the marriage. Which goes back to what my friend Bob Zellinger said: communication is paramount to making a marriage successful. You need to be open and explicit with your partner about what you expect, whether you are happy or not, particularly in regard to the relationship itself.

Money can be another divisive issue in marriage. Rick sees two financial themes: one, someone in the marriage is not making enough money; and two, someone in the marriage is *spending* too much money.

I'm not going to drill in on this topic further because I discuss finances fully in other sections of the book. The only concept I will emphasize here is that, when dealing with financial issues in a marriage, there needs to be common goals, expectations, and strategies. If there's no alignment, you will experience stress.

Rick proposes that partners in the marriage do periodic check-ins to assess how things are going. This will make the partnership more successful. Personally, Rick does a monthly self-check-in on the eleventh of every month, the date of his birthday. Rick thinks about how he is doing as a husband, what he did right and wrong over the past thirty days, and how he can try to be better. Additionally, he performs the same review for his roles as a father, lawyer, and individual. This monthly practice helps Rick stay on track as a husband, and in his other roles too.

Finally, Rick encourages adopting the Serenity Prayer:

God, grant me the serenity to accept the things I cannot change;
Courage to change the things I can;
And wisdom to know the difference.

In marriage, focusing too much time and energy on what you cannot change will end with frustration and disappointment. You absolutely do not have the ability to change everything, only what you can control. Focus on that.

PUT YOUR SPOUSE FIRST

Again, I'm truly lucky. After twenty-four years of marriage, I actually love Mom more now than when we married.

As our marriage has developed and evolved, we've shared more experiences, both good and bad, that makes us a team in a way we could have never foreseen before marriage. There is a deeper sense of trust, shared responsibility, and caring.

More than likely, your spouse will be your very best friend and the most important person in your world. Marriage will be a source of emotional support, companionship, and comfort. You must never take marriage for granted. To make it successful you need to constantly tend to the garden and remove the weeds that inevitably encroach. If you regularly perfect a marriage—through honest, open communication, flexibility, and the willingness to find the right mix of growing together while giving each other independent space—it can thrive and flourish. If you let the weeds enter and multiply, the marriage will atrophy and fail.

Mutual respect is what many call it. It goes back to Judy Bernstein's attribute list, and the capacity to remember and embrace kindness. A simple key to any relationship, including marriage, is listening, actively listening to your partner. Not being emotionally and mentally present when your partner is talking is disrespectful and will create resentment.

Think of it this way: when you get married, you're signing up for a long-term partnership. A partnership often implies a fifty-fifty relationship, but that doesn't need to be the case. To make sure your marriage is on the right track, do not seek an equal partnership—seek a seventy-thirty partnership, where you are the seventy. In other words, do more, give more, and be more. If you're lucky enough to be in a marriage where both partners seek to be a seventy percent partner, the marriage is more likely to thrive and grow over time.

Jon Hotchkiss takes it a step further. Once you get married, put your spouse first; give of yourself without expecting anything in return. It's good for you and your relationship—and it's good for your soul.

WRAP UP

A healthy marriage is absolutely wonderful and tremendously fun. It even extends your life (researchers found the risk of death was 32 percent higher across a lifetime for single men compared to married men. Single women face a 23 percent higher mortality risk, compared to married women).[17] A bad marriage must be completely miserable. Fortunately, I do not know. To make your marriage a success, pick the right partner and then do everything possible to feed and invest in the relationship. Expect change. Take responsibility. Give more than you get.

CAREER

Selecting your career is the second biggest decision of your life, after deciding whom you will marry. Despite the significance of the decision, you are not your career, and you are not what you do. Still, your work can provide you with wonderful meaning, satisfaction, and joy.

When you think about it, you spend many a waking hour each day engaged in your career. One way to know you've made a great choice is if you wake up on a regular basis with enthusiasm and energy, looking forward to your work. You might find time zipping by, as you are engrossed in your work. This is sometimes referred to as a state of flow—a concept featured in Mihaly Csikszentmihalyi's book, *Flow: The Psychology of Optimal Experience*. Conversely, if you dread getting out of bed and time languishes, you are most decidedly in the wrong place.

Royce Yudkoff frames the career question this way: "What do you choose to do to make 75 percent of your waking hours satisfying?" This question is meant to encourage a focus on having a well-rounded life; to not be a careerist, but to get the work question as right as possible from the get-go. Part of a successful career is to deliberately think about what will give you satisfaction.

I'll say this frequently: life is about meaningful satisfaction and happiness. I define meaningful satisfaction as believing the activities you are engaged in positively impact your community in some way and make you feel good as well—that what you do as a person, personally and professionally, is valued and you enjoy doing it. Your job and career can certainly enhance or detract from that objective but, life is not about work. Work should fit into your life and your life should not necessarily orbit around your work. I cannot emphasize this enough.

When I ran my company, work excessively dominated my life. It wasn't good. I may have been at many a soccer game, but on the phone dealing with business. I was physically present, but mentally absent. This behavior was not being honest with you or myself. I was trying to be a good dad by being at the soccer game, but I was not fully there.

I know I'm not alone. John Kenny, former CFO of Iron Mountain, admits he often arrived home from work to sit in his garage, on the phone finishing a business conversation, while his wife and children were inside the house.

Me at the soccer game, John in his garage, signals to the most important people in our lives that something is more important than they are, which is not true. I'm sure you saw me on the phone at soccer games and I regret not fully focusing on what was important at that moment: you. You were just too nice to say something about it.

Make sure your life has balance. Work is part of it, but not the whole of it. Your lifestyle should be able to include being healthy by engaging in regular exercise, investing in and enjoying personal relationships and friendships, not bearing excessive stress, not traveling for business to the point where you forget where you are when you wake up (this has happened to me many times).

With that in mind, understand how your career will impact your desired lifestyle: will you be working long hours; will you travel extensively; will you have ample free time to pursue your interests outside of work, including maintaining important relationships? Also, try to understand that work travel is far less glamorous and interesting than it sounds. It gets old very quickly and usually allows for little free time. It certainly is not a vacation.

How much money you might earn is an important decision when considering a job but it should not dominate your thought process. No amount of money is worth being miserable, and you probably need a lot less of it than you might think to be happy. Too often people make decisions that revolve around money in the short term and wind up disappointed in the long term. Of course, how much you earn matters, but think carefully about how money impacts your decision-making.

NOT TOO HARD, NOT TOO SOFT

When you think about a career, you should consider many things: what interests you or what you enjoy; what you will actually do every day; how the career will impact your lifestyle; and how much money you'll make.

Getting established professionally takes years and it can be difficult to switch roads once launched, without taking many steps backward. So you'll want to choose well.

You should also think about how you best thrive and in what type of structure you can be most successful. Some industries and organizations mimic academic environments in that they tend to move in annual progression-like steps—a small promotion or step up each year. Many professional service organizations adopt this model: accounting, consulting, and banking. Other industries are far more free form and do not have the same rhythm. Hollywood is a great example of this—teams smash together for a specific project, like a movie, then disband once complete.

You will probably have a preference or distaste for a certain type of organization. Furthermore, you should consider whether you want to be part of a very large company with thousands or tens of thousands of people, or if you would prefer a smaller company. There is no right answer; you just need to find what's best for you and your style.

But it is important you find the right fit. You could be an absolutely wonderful consultant in a large multi-national organization that draws upon your skills perfectly, but if you find yourself in a small business you might not be playing to your strengths at all. Think about the context in which you will play.

Of course, you can experiment with multiple types of businesses and discover what works best for you. And best of all, all experiences will help shape you and refine what that is.

SOME PASSIONS ARE BETTER LEFT AS PASSIONS

When choosing your career, you might naturally gravitate towards something that appeals to you or captivates your interest. You're passionate about skiing and might find yourself wanting to work in the ski industry. This is absolutely fine, but you should also consider whether your passions are good sources of employment or good businesses.

I'm not encouraging you to be overly practical, just to consider the reality that some passions are better left as passions, not turned into careers.

To clarify, you should be aware of all of the positive and negative consequences of the career choices you make. For example, if you choose to be a ski instructor, you might love that career because you get to be outside with active people doing something you enjoy. But, you might not earn the salary you want or need. It's not that you must immediately dismiss being a ski instructor; you simply need to make sure you'll be happy with both the pros and cons of that career. And if you decide it won't make a good career, just make sure the career you do choose, allows time for your recreational passions.

Again, I'm not proposing that you abandon your interests when thinking about a career; just think about your options holistically.

UNDERSTAND THE DAY-TO-DAY REALITY OF WHAT YOU'LL DO

Sometimes young people have a vision of what a job or career entails. Sometimes that vision is shaped by a television show or a movie and is overly influenced by the very best parts of a job. Try to understand exactly what a job or career really involves; what you really do on a daily basis.

Many positions, no matter how glamorous they sound, are about sitting at a desk, working on a computer, and talking on a phone. Good or bad, it's the reality of the job. So make a point of understanding what you will really do. *There are a lot of meetings*—super, if you love lots of meetings. *If it entails writing a lot of memos or reports*—wonderful, if you enjoy writing memos and reports. You need to know these things; because on the flip-side, if you don't enjoy those tasks, they'll make you unhappy.

As far as that mix of glamour and pedestrian work go, think of a professional football player. Game day is Sunday; and it's filled with lots of adulation and excitement—the glamour moment. Monday through Saturday is all about practice, film study, stretching, strength training, visioning, and recuperation. Not bad ways to spend your time, but certainly not the adrenaline rush of Sunday. Try to understand what the mix of prep and game day is in any career you are evaluating. No career is all game day. Be aware that most of the time you are practicing and preparing for rare exciting moments.

Once you focus in on your particular job, try to project yourself into an organization or career track and understand the culture and norms you're signing up for. Mari Kuraishi, founder and CEO of Global Giving, faced a pivot point in her career, when she slammed against a culture she was ill-suited for. After leaving the World Bank, Mari considered going into investment banking. She interviewed at a handful of investment banks; what appealed to her was the emerging markets work the banks were doing in Eastern Europe, her area of expertise and focus. What she didn't like was the culture. She perceived that the investment banks were exclusively focused on their own profits and were not thinking about how to help their clients or build more stable markets in Eastern Europe. Feeling disenchanted, Mari decided this was not a match for her.

Please note, neither Mari nor I are saying the investment banks were wrong for their priorities—that's their choice. Mari was simply self-aware enough to know what she wanted. She was asking herself the right questions about what she could expect down the road.

This is another reason why understanding your values, what works for you, what doesn't, will allow you to safeguard your happiness. This understanding will serve as an excellent filter when faced with such choices.

Also, jobs and careers morph over time. Try to look into the future and see what it holds when you are thirty, forty, or fifty. Talk to people in your chosen field who are older and appear successful. Are they happy? Are they married? Do they engage with their children? Are they healthy? Before you chase something, try to understand what it will look like and feel like if you achieve it.

In his early twenties, entrepreneur Jason Pananos worked at United Technologies, the large Hartford-based conglomerate; he looked ahead by studying the lives of the senior executives there. While appealing, at least in some aspects, their existences made him realize he wanted a life where he had more control over his own destiny and more contact with employees and customers. This led him to opt out of a corporate career and do something more entrepreneurial. (When I was younger, I also highly valued control, independence, and the ability to make changes as I saw fit. This led me in an entrepreneurial direction.)

I know many fifty-year-olds who are professionally successful by most definitions, but they're not happy, married, healthy, or close with their children. I would not wish that on anybody. So, before you set out on a course, try to understand what the waypoints and destinations look like; you might be surprised. When you're young, this is very challenging to do, but I encourage you to try. If you set upon a course that does not provide happiness, while it might be difficult, you can change.

To discover what a job actually entails, simply ask people who work that particular job. As Jon Hotchkiss points out, most people are absolutely thrilled to talk about themselves and what they do. Try contacting people in fields you are interested in; ask them for a brief, thirty-minute meeting—over coffee, at the office, or by phone. Then ask questions like:

- What do you like most about your job?

- What do you like least about your job?

- How did you wind up in the role you are in?

- What do you spend most of your time doing in your day?

- What do you wish you could do more of in your job?

Many aspiring entrepreneurs contact me asking for my advice on how to build a business. I don't think I have ever said no to someone who wanted to speak with me. Perhaps Jon is correct in that I'm happy to satisfy my own ego by prattling away; but I like to think I'm giving back and helping someone who is thinking about traveling the same path I chose. Either way, the aspiring entrepreneur has a bit more information and insight into the career to which they intend to devote themselves.

SKATE TO WHERE THE PUCK IS GOING

This is where the benefit of a long-term, multi-decade perspective really kicks in. Resist the temptation to do something safe when you are young at the expense of something that will actually get you to where you want to be as you get older. This is a lot like what the famous hockey player, Wayne Gretzky, means when he says he likes to "skate to where the puck is going, not where it has been."

Think about jobs and careers in light of where the puck is going, not where it has been.

Here's an example: Royce Yudkoff admits that choosing to be a lawyer, an appealing career for some, is not something he would choose or advise anybody to choose, despite its ease of entry for a young person. The path is so well oiled, so well-defined—college, law school, entry-level job, the big law firm—it's easy to find yourself on it even though it leads you someplace you don't necessarily want to go. In Royce's eyes, being a lawyer is not where the puck is going, it's where the puck is.

Many end up in careers ill-suited for them the same way—by following the path of least resistance, the tried and true way, with zero thought as to what will make them happy down the road.

At one time or another, we're all guilty of being persuaded to follow a larger group, or giving in to the tug and pressure of our environment. It's like a gravitational pull.

Rachel Albert is familiar with that pull. While in college, she initially wanted to pursue a career in law. But after some time, she realized social service was the right match for her. At Amherst, where she was studying, social services were not as large a focus as certain pre-professional tracks, like law. Yet, Rachel refused to let the environment and culture dissuade her from what she thought was the right fit for her.

Even though she socializes with many people in law, finance, or business, Rachel still feels social service was the right path for her. Take her lead. Know where you want to go and look ahead; if your chosen path gets you to where you want to go, it will be worth it—even if you sense that others look askance at your choice.

GO WHERE THE TALENT IS NOT

Go where the talent is not. I find it fascinating that young people gravitate towards glamorous industries deep with talent. Perhaps it's because the path is so well trod. Perhaps it's where the proverbial puck lies. I am sure these industries offer a great work environment and a sort of satisfying challenge, but it's much harder to excel in an environment bloated with super people.

Before you make a decision, think about being in an industry that has a great business model (this is crucially important), but is not overly populated with amazing people. To use a simple sports analogy, I'd prefer to play basketball with a seven-foot hoop rather than a ten-foot hoop; it's just easier.

You see, every year many young adults pour into the worlds of technology and finance seeking careers and success. While this is not a bad choice, these fields have tons of astonishingly talented and gritty people. This is clearly a ten-foot-hoop situation, maybe even a twelve–foot-hoop. Of course, if your heart is in one of those fields, you should absolutely go there. Just know the odds of success might not be tilted in the right direction because of the deep talent pool. Alternatively, entering into a field where the talent pool is not as deep, the people, not as gritty, is akin to the seven-foot hoop: it is just easier to play in that game.

Now finding great business models without a deep talent pool is challenging, but it is achievable—and if you can locate such an opportunity the result can be powerful.

Take Jason Pananos and Jay Davis, for example. After completing business school, they rejected the normal banking and finance career paths and instead found and purchased a small business in Little Rock, Arkansas, in the commercial pest industry. Their business is not the residential pest control model that may initially come to mind; rather, their business helps municipalities control pest issues on a wide scale community basis. Using mitigants, they control air and water borne risks that could negatively impact a community or region.

Jason and Jay went to play their game on a low hoop, in a great industry. Their industry is not populated with overly talented and ambitious people. They have created a wonderful business and lifestyle for themselves by seeking out a game in which they can use their innate talents, their grit, in a low hoop context.

So, think about where and how you would like to build your career. Then consider how you might find an amazing business model going into a low hoop game.

PUT YOURSELF IN THE WAY OF LUCK

You can position yourself for luck in many ways. If you place yourself in a spot where lots of ideas, people, and opportunities cross paths with you, you might tend to be luckier, simply because you can act on those opportunities.

Certain professions, for instance, tend to be a crossroads of sorts. Lawyers tend to see a lot of people, ideas, and opportunities. Certain types of professors see lots of new technologies, meet interesting people, and come in contact with thought-provoking ideas. You can almost think of this positioning as a lookout post where you can get a glimpse of many things and judiciously select when to act. This type of positioning can make you luckier.[18]

The same is true with friendships. If you put yourself in a spot where you see and interact with many people, you can choose the best matches for you. Being involved in clubs and organizations in college and post-college brings you into connection with people and you will have a deeper pool of potential friends and relationships.

It's all connected—you just need to get to a place where you can see it.

BE PART OF SOMETHING BIGGER THAN YOU

What will make you happy down the road? That's the question. For many, an important part of work is to be part of something greater than themselves, of serving a purpose, and supporting a mission bigger than them.

Andrew Roberts is a nonprofit professional based in Columbus, Ohio. After graduating from Harvard Business School, he initially followed a fairly traditional corporate track. His first job was with a company whose primary strategy was to shut down factories and fire employees. *Wow, how would that make you feel every day?* No surprise; Andrew didn't enjoy that type of work. His next position was at a rapidly growing public company, where employees had to best themselves every quarter.

These experiences left him feeling hollow; they did not make him feel part of something larger and more purposeful.

When I first met Andrew, he was the Executive Director of the YMCA where I exercised. The first time I entered his office, I saw a huge collage of airline boarding passes on the wall. Curious, I asked Andrew what they were all about and he told me "work travel." Andrew had saved every single airline boarding pass from his previous jobs and kept them framed and visible as a reminder of what his life was like, why those jobs had not been right for him or his family. The boarding pass collage reminded him of his former life and why he was far happier in the social services world. Not only did he enjoy life balance, because he was not voraciously traveling, but he was part of an organization with a mission and purpose he believed in. He was part of a team where something was being accomplished that was greater than his individual self. At fifty, Andrew is not a new age millennial, but he shares with them this deep desire for purpose and mission.

Feeling part of an organization you believe in—one that is bigger and better than its individual members—is very satisfying. Much like being part of a sports team; if your team works well together, it's rewarding, regardless of the individual role you play. You're allocating your time and energy to something that has more meaning than compensation, where you truly feel committed and engaged. This is a wonderful feeling and is only surpassed by leading such an organization.

UNDERSTANDING COMPENSATION

OK, let's talk about money. Obviously, this is one of the factors you'll need to consider when evaluating a career option. Again, as I have stressed, this is not the only consideration, but it is an important one.

When working, you can typically earn money in two forms: earned income and equity. Earned income is typically compensation for your labor; equity is a form of ownership. Most people I have known accumulate money and wealth through equity and not earned income. These are people who own their own businesses or have equity interests in larger corporations where they work. So, if you do want money, position yourself for equity more than earned income.

Typically, compensation for labor is capped—you can

only rise so far before you hit the ceiling. Ownership opportunities, on the other hand, are uncapped. In most industries, it's the owners, or equity holders, that reap the financial rewards, not the employees who work for them. There are a few exceptions where earned income can trump equity. In Hollywood, professional sports, and on Wall Street, you can earn vast sums of money without having an equity stake.

When you own a business you tend to have capital (money) and an organizational system working for you to create value and wealth. One way to think about this is you can be earning and creating wealth whether you are physically working or not. This is because the system is working for you whether you are there or not. Contrast this to an employee who is part of the system and working for earned income: that employee only earns if he is actually working.

Consider my dad, who was a dentist—which is not quite having equity and not quite being an employee, it's being self-employed. My dad would often tell me that the only time he was earning money was if he had a patient in a chair and his hands were in their mouth. Not exactly a pretty picture, but the point was clear: if he was not in his office plying his trade, he was not making money.

So, whether you choose to own a business or work for a business, get as much equity as you can. Often employees can participate in a company's equity by purchasing it, getting equity options (stocks or shares), and being given equity as part of the compensation package.

When thinking about compensation, resist the temptation to make short-term decisions. What you initially get paid does not really matter compared to the long-term opportunities available. Again, you want to see the whole game, not just a single inning.

Jason Pananos says it really doesn't matter what you get paid in your early to mid-twenties. This era is all about learning and gathering experiences that will help you refine what exactly it is you want to do, propel you down the road, and afford you the opportunity to meet and surround yourself with interesting and smart people. These are all much more important considerations than current income in your early twenties, which will not really vary that much. By focusing on people, experiences and learning, Jason believes you can position yourself for the entire game instead of the early innings.

Ken Saxon echoes Jason's thoughts. Ken went to work for Trammell Crow, a national real estate firm in Dallas, Texas, after college and before business school. Ken chose his first job based on the opportunity to learn as much as possible and see as much as he could. Ken did not care or think about monetary compensation at that job. Learning and education was the compensation he cared the most about.

The key, in terms of money: if you're successful at what you do, chances are good you will make plenty of money over time.

HOW TO BEHAVE IN A JOB

- Be on time for work—better yet, be early.

- Remember, your employer needs to make money from your labor.

- Ask how you can be helpful or do a better job.

- You will have customers. Customers can be external users of your company or internal people within the company. Make sure you are doing the very best job possible for your customers.

- Be respectful and polite to everybody you encounter.

- Learn as much as you can about your job and the jobs of other people.

- Try to understand how the entire company works.

- Take notes on what you learn and observe, which will allow you develop your own style.

- See how various people act and behave. This is an opportunity for you to learn and model. Try to develop your own style and habits based on what you see. Take and amalgamate what you like and reject what you do not like.

THE TORTOISE AND THE HARE

Remember Aesop's famous fable *The Tortoise and The Hare*? The hare's challenged to a race by the tortoise. The tortoise slowly yet doggedly progresses along his path, while the hare darts off at the start, only to stop for a nap along the way. As we all know, the tortoise wins the race thanks to his slow but steady progression. The story is about a simple race, yet it serves as a metaphor for finding happiness, success, and satisfaction in life.

What makes for a successful career? I'm not sure there's an easy answer to that question; I'm not even sure I'm qualified to opine, but I'll share my intuition.

First, I think people who rise to important positions within organizations stay and embrace the marathon race. In the book *Outliers,* Malcolm Gladwell talks about needing 10,000 hours to develop mastery in something. Building a career requires this kind of time, too. Individuals must put the time in and endure and take positions of increasing importance and responsibilities over a few decades. Their progression is tortoise-like, but consistent, and they remain in a single industry, perhaps in a single company, and build a reputation, expertise, and a track record of achievement. When other people get fatigued or bored and bolt from a company, they stay and power on, taking on larger and larger roles. They win through endurance and staying power over long periods of time. Grit is so important (so much so that I have devoted an entire chapter to it).

Rarely do people have meteoric ascension in their careers. Sometimes, when people try to force the acceleration of their progression, they act like the periphrastic hare, jumping from one place to the next, lurching into new starts and sidesteps without making significant progression, but expending significant energy along the way.

I've said it before, and I'll say it again: slow and steady wins the race and endurance is the game. There are rarely overnight successes, although we all want to believe they exist.

An article in the *Huffington Post* illuminates this concept well.[18] Dustin Moskovitz, one of the founders of ubiquitous Facebook, was asked about the social media company's overnight success. His reply: "If by 'overnight success' you mean staying up and coding all night, every night for six years straight, then it felt quite tiring and stressful." The article continues to point out that it is the little things that matter and get you to the big things.

Doing something (like writing code) relentlessly over years gets you to the polished, finished product. In the end, it may appear hare-like, like it happened seemingly overnight, but it's the tortoise-like pursuit—often unnoticed—over time, that leads to that big outcome.

IT'S ALL ABOUT RELATIONSHIPS

People who thrive tend to have very strong people skills. They have the ability to attract, influence, and lead people in a constructive and collaborative way. They might not have the best technical skills, but they get along well with people, they're likable, and work well with diverse groups. Of course, if someone has both technical skills and people skills, all the better. So, if I could just pick one, I would pick the people skills.

This is something Jon Hotchkiss did not fully understand

after college; it took him time to figure out. You see, Jon works in the entertainment industry in Hollywood. Structured a bit more like project work, people come together for a production and then disband when the project is over. Therefore, people are constantly being reshuffled for projects and people get tapped and recruited through relationships.

Over time, Jon came to see that in a world without a specific hierarchy, relationships are the key determinant in progress and advancement. When relationships are so crucial, it's truly important to get along with as many people as possible and to be perceived as a person who is cooperative and a team player. "Nobody likes the guy who taints the well," he points out.

It's important to note, people skills include the ability to be receptive to and good at taking input and feedback from others. It can be challenging if you're a person who is overly committed to your own ideas and perspective; it can be difficult not to take it personally, but it's important.

Lastly, stay a people person. It seems like it should go without saying, but it's amazing how often people are not nice to people as their careers advance. But there's a reason for the tired cliché: be nice to everybody on the way up, because you'll see them on the way down too. It's true.

YOU WILL HAVE MULTIPLE CAREERS

At the risk of contradicting myself, here's a thought that should take the pressure off: it used to be, you would select a career and be engaged in that profession, with that company, for a lifetime. That's no longer the case. You should expect to have multiple careers, jobs, and employers in your life. This means, if you make a mistake, or finish a chapter in your career, you can switch gears and no one will accuse you of being whimsical. Not that you should be concerned with what other people think.

A career that has many twists and turns will allow you to gain skills and experiences that are transferable across different industries and companies. It can make your life more interesting. Even if you stay in the same profession, you can grow within a profession and expand it to take on new roles.

In addition, work seems to be shifting to a 'gig' based model where you are effectively self-employed and engage in multiple projects concurrently or sequentially—think Uber driver.

Starting a new chapter in your career can be invigorating and stimulating. Changing your role, geography, or company is a way to re-energize your career. Mixing up your career arc is a way to force you to grow and develop and avoid the comfort of being in the same place for too long. It's easy to grow stale if you cling to the comfort zone.

Even if you do stay in the same place, it's very possible to reinvent your role periodically, as you and the organization mature and develop.

CHAPTER BY CHAPTER

Another way to think about it: your career has different chapters, each with a different emphasis and focus.

Think of Ken Saxon, who saw his first job—his first chapter, as it were—as an opportunity to learn, and not earn.

Similarly, Royce Yudkoff's career philosophy is oriented around learning, earning, and returning. He spent the first part of his career absorbing and learning as much as he could; synthesizing information and experiences as he better defined his professional direction. The next chapter was about monetizing the learning phase. Royce recently entered the returning chapter, where he shifted from an emphasis of earning to returning by becoming a teacher. He now helps new groups of young people as they enter their learning years, thereby continuing the cycle, fueling regeneration.

Mom and I think of ourselves in the returning phase,

being teachers and helping young people launch their lives.

It's a nice way to think about the career arc, having different priorities at different moments. There is something very appealing and satisfying about shifting into a returning mode at some point.

Returning can take many forms, but principally it's about giving back, helping others, and making the world better in some way. Although there's no right or wrong, it does seem less fulfilling if you become successful, only to stay in the earning mode forever, never shifting into the returning chapter.

A SIDEBAR ON BEING AN ENTREPRENEUR

When thinking about career choices, please consider being an entrepreneur—which is just a fancy word for being your own boss. Running your own business, whether you start it or buy it, can be incredibly satisfying and fulfilling. Of course, it's challenging and fraught with difficulty, but it's yours in every way.

Working at a large company provides stability and a predictable path at times, but it can be bureaucratic, too. It might be difficult to implement change. Often, you're doing what you're told and following a predetermined path. You can be limited to a small area or function within the larger picture. This can potentially be less satisfying because you're a small cog in a big system.

Running a business, on the other hand, lets you see the entire picture and implement change or your ideas at your own pace.

When running a business, I would often contemplate challenges, opportunities, and solutions over the weekend and, come Monday morning, I would jump right in with experimentation and implementation (after thought, analysis, and consideration, mind you). This was very satisfying. I enjoyed a direct connection between my thought process and creative implementation.

If you work in a large organization, your career can be random and subject to the division you're in; the level of success of your boss; whether you click with superiors; whether the entire company thrives or implodes.

Outwardly, a bigger company may have the patina of stability, but if you scratch a few layers, there's a ton of risk—risk that might be in a different form than that experienced by an entrepreneur, but risk all the same.

In my interviews, a consistent theme was the desire for independence and control in life. Royce Yudkoff said, "I wanted a high level of independence; I did not want someone controlling my life."

Royce founded a very successful investment firm in Boston, ABRY Partners. Full disclosure, I had the privilege of working with Royce when ABRY was an investor, and a fantastic one, in ArchivesOne. This entrepreneurial venture, ABRY, gave Royce the opportunity for independence and control.

Danny Rosen, a childhood friend who's currently a professor at the University of Pittsburgh, shared that his father, Yudi, gave him two pieces of advice that deeply impacted him. One theme focused on marriage; and the other focused on being your own boss.

Being your own boss can mean a lot of things. To Danny, who thinks he has the best job in the world, he feels like he's his own boss even though his position is not classically thought of as such. As a professor, Danny gets to do the research he chooses and teach the classes he chooses. In his mind, he has a very high degree of time independence.

Danny's father, on the other hand, worked his entire life at one company, a prominent jewelry business in Manhattan. (A quick tangent: Danny's father, Yudi Rosen, was the very first person to know I was going to ask your mom to marry me. I purchased the engagement ring from him!) Yudi initially liked working at the business, but that morphed when the namesake founder died and the business changed ownership and leadership. Yudi progressed into being the Chief Financial Officer as his career evolved, but he was not happy. His work no longer gave him joy or satisfaction. Danny learned from this and made sure he selected a career trajectory that gave him independence and delight.

Two of your grandparents and three of your great-grandparents were entrepreneurs and business owners. I am not pretending that this is some type of family legacy or mantle you must carry, just sharing an interesting fact.

It's rare that I hear people say they really want to work for someone else and have less control in their lives. As I have indicated, being an entrepreneur, or your own boss, has plenty of risks, but many super advantages.

When you're an entrepreneur you feel a bit like an architect designing a building. You also get operating leverage—people working for you to make the business bigger, better, and more valuable. Finally, being an entrepreneur is a great form of equity accumulation (this is a fancy way of saying that the potential exists to make some money), if you're successful and lucky.

When you think about entrepreneurship, do not limit your scope to software and technology concepts that are popularized in the media. This is one of those overcrowded pools of talent I mentioned previously. Again, I'm not saying those are bad choices at all, but the world of entrepreneurship is broad and can include all types of businesses that are mundane, not unlike Jason and Jay's pest control endeavor.

If you're an entrepreneur, building and making the business excellent—not necessarily the business product or service itself—is exciting enough. I have many entrepreneurial friends who are in thriving, successful businesses that at first glance do not appear to be that exciting.

Brad Morris is one example. He runs a business that sells

and services machines that manufacture part components— not exactly an initial image of dynamism. Brad's business employs approximately 700 people and operates throughout the world. Brad has all the excitement, and challenges, he could want with his business.

Parker Davis runs a large, regional telephone answering service—Answer1, in Phoenix, Arizona—that's growing, doing very well, and providing Parker with great opportunities for himself and his family.

You can be an entrepreneur in any type of industry or business and sometimes the very best and most exciting opportunities are those that are a bit off the radar screen. So, if being an entrepreneur appeals to you, keep your mind open to all sorts of businesses and ideas. If you're interested in the topic, you'll find some relevant books in the Suggested Reading section.

Lastly, being an entrepreneur when young is the best because you have nothing to lose. If you start early enough, you are not yet in the more risk adverse mode that accompanies having a mortgage, family, and high responsibility. Although you lack some experience, you have boundless energy and enthusiasm—which is often undervalued. I would just about always trade experience for a smart, incredibly hungry, and energetic person. Sometimes experience is bad experience, so the notion of waiting to be an entrepreneur so you have more experience can be a mistake in logic. And if you fail, you can always reorient and recover.

In short, never underestimate the joy of running your own show. When you're young may be the best time to see for yourself.

ONE MORE YEAR OF WORK WILL BE JUST THAT

The real job you'll face is figuring out what your path will be. Please do not have any preconceived notions about what you're supposed to do or be. This is your path and you can do whatever makes you happy and brings you satisfaction. I will encourage you to slow the action down, pause, breathe, so you can better connect with what it is that you want for your life, who you want to be.

Maybe you will come out of college wanting to be a lawyer, or a nonprofit leader, like Andrew; who knows? When you think about your career, just realize you can do anything you want to do.

A friend once confided that he felt like he had to get on with his life in a very specific way—working for a large corporation—once he graduated from college. He wishes he had delayed getting a job and done something like the Peace Corps, rather than jumping right into a career. When he did launch his career, it was at a bank. Looking back, he now wishes he had taken more risk and done something with smaller companies. Such a move would have been far more satisfying.

There's no rush. Do something unique or special right after college and you might have a memory and experience that can last a lifetime. One more year of work will be just that. A year or two in the Peace Corps or a similar program will likely be something you can hold in your heart and mind forever.

WRAP UP

When you choose a career, remember that I love you no matter what and will be proud of you regardless of your choice. I want you to be happy and fulfilled. You can be whatever you choose. Whatever it is, I hope you find passion and excellence. If I can leave you with one more thought, it's this: do not dismiss luck in career success. Being in the right place at the right time can be serendipity, but it does play a large role in careers and people's success. So get out there, build lasting relationships, and experience all you can.

MONEY AND FINANCE

Let me pause for a moment, before we dive deeper into this topic. I don't want to overestimate the importance of money in your life. I promise you, money alone will not make you happy or bring you satisfaction. I know far too many wealthy people who seem unhappy. That said, I'd rather be financially comfortable than not.

It's very important for you to have control over your finances. Financial stress is an awful feeling and it's usually avoidable.

If you're lucky and smart enough to accumulate some money somewhere along the way in life, do not confuse this achievement with being better than anybody else. I know plenty of people with money who are not nice people and I know plenty of people without much money who are generally decent. Having money just means you have some money; it doesn't mean you're inherently better, smarter, or anything else. You would be surprised how many people do not understand this simple concept.

How you view money, and manage it, is an important

decision in life. So much of wealth accumulation comes down to choice.

A FOOL'S GAME

In Greek mythology, the parable of Icarus depicts hubris, wanting too much and being overly ambitious. As Icarus soars too high and too close to the sun, disregarding his father's warnings, his wax wings melt, and he tragically falls to the sea. It serves as a warning to us all: resist the temptation to desire more for the sake of having more. When our appetites are endless, we risk the fate of Icarus.

Money is a tool and a means; nothing more, nothing less. The constant pursuit of more stuff, which is so prevalent in our culture, is a fool's game.

A classic financial definition of money is that it's a store of value, which can be exchanged for use at some point in the future. Money should not be a goal unto itself. Rather, the goal should be that which money gives you the ability to do. Chasing something that's infinite will result in always wanting more.

My friend and mentor, Tom Bird, thinks about money in terms of enough or not enough. (You can apply this screen to both income and assets—but it's always better to have an asset mindset as compared to an income mindset.)

Here's what he means.

If you need a certain amount of money per month to cover your savings goal, living expenses, and all taxes, and you have an income greater than that (with some safety margin), you are in great shape and you do not need to be overly absorbed in thinking about your financial situation. You are in balance and equilibrium. You have enough.

Similarly, if you have a savings goal of a certain amount, you achieve it, and you can live off the savings and the income that savings generates, you are in a fantastic spot and once again, you do not need to spend too much of your precious time and brain cells focusing on financial issues (although you absolutely still have to monitor it). Again, you have enough.

On the other hand, if you do not have enough money for your current needs or savings goals, you need to stay focused and understand what is preventing you from achieving your goals, or how much more time you need to get to where you want to be.

Tom asserts that when you clearly understand what your needs and goals are in this arena, the measuring stick is very simple and binary: you either have enough or not enough (relative to your goals and needs).

Once you have enough, you can fill your life and time with whatever you choose. You don't need to chase more money—which can be an unwinnable game.

Tom's simple screen is a great way to emphasize that money is a tool to serve you, not something you should chase without bounds or constraints.

Remember, money itself rarely brings you happiness. I have more money now than I did in my thirties, but I'm not sure that I'm fundamentally happier (I am not unhappier, either). People and experiences will bring you joy in life, so focus on those things and do not chase money.

SOME PRINCIPLES FOR FINANCIAL SUCCESS

So, how do you get to a point where you have enough money? You not only earn it; you manage it well.

Let me introduce you to some simple principles for financial success.

- **Spend less than you earn**. The simplest way to condense money issues is to spend less than you earn. Jim Ratliff, a successful entrepreneur and investor, insists that young people should spend way less than they earn so there's a significant margin of safety, as well as an opportunity for investment. Although it might be difficult for you to imagine, many people continually spend more than they earn. How is it possible to spend more than you earn? Unfortunately, it's easy if you choose to accumulate debt. If you continually spend less than you earn—and consistently salt away savings for the future—you will likely be in a good place. This might seem simple, but temptations lurk everywhere.

- **Stay off the credit treadmill.** When you're in college, you will receive a plethora of offers for credit cards. Reject them. This is their attempt to get you on the credit treadmill. You need only one or two credit cards, not a collection of them.

- **Track your spending**. Controlling your spending is the single most important part of your financial health. Most people don't do this and dramatically underestimate their spending. Not tracking your spending is a bit like not knowing how much gas you have in your car—you're driving blind. It might be helpful for you to use a program like Mint, Personal Capital, or Quicken to help track your spending. These software programs automatically track your spending by linking to your bank and credit card accounts, summarizing all the numbers in one easy-to-read report. Once the information is automatically gathered you will be able to see trends over time and by category. This will give you the information and tools to make enlightened and improved decisions.

- **It's not the big things that get you**. When you think about spending, don't be tricked into thinking that the big, rare expenses are the challenge. These types of expenses can certainly be problematic, but it's often the small, innocuous expenses over time that are a problem.

Take a coffee drinker who spends five dollars a day on a small indulgence at their local coffee shop, just to get the day going. This seemingly immaterial expense adds up to $1,825 per year and $18,250 over a ten-year period. That certainly feels like a lot of money to me.

- **Have an emergency fund**. Many people choose to live paycheck to paycheck, spending all their take-home pay each pay period, because they don't make building up savings a priority. Often the phenomenon of living paycheck to paycheck is perceived as a low-income problem. I don't believe that's fully accurate. People who earn high incomes can also live paycheck to paycheck, just at a more luxurious level. People can encumber themselves with mortgages on fancy homes, car payments, and indulgent lifestyles. Living paycheck to paycheck means, if you don't receive your next paycheck, you'll have a problem very quickly.

  But if you build savings, you can withstand a temporary setback and tolerate a handful of skipped paychecks.

  To get started, one of your first financial goals might be to accumulate an emergency savings fund—an account you can only tap into if you face a setback. To build your fund, on a monthly basis you might add a fixed dollar amount or a percentage of your monthly earnings, say 15 percent of your take home total.

- **Pay your bills on time**. Not only is paying your

bills on time the right thing to do, it will impact your credit score, a measure of your creditworthiness. You'll receive better service when you pay your bills on time. Service providers will return your calls quicker if you pay your bills on time.

- **Keep it simple.** I know people with multiple credit cards, multiple bank accounts, multiple investment accounts, and scores of individual investment holdings. I'm not sure why this is the case, but it creates complexity. It involves more time and bandwidth to administer; and it can be avoided. I manage to exist with two credit cards, one bank account, and one investment account. It keeps things straightforward and simple. Some people boast of many mutual funds, or oodles of stocks, in multiple investment accounts. It looks like a grab bag of decisions or a chronology of herky-jerky ideas over time. In comparison, I have about six mutual funds in our Vanguard account—and I could probably get down to three if I wanted to. In finance, like all parts of your life, simple usually is superior to complex. Simple is easy to understand and administer and gives you a sense of calm. Best of all, simplicity allows you to focus on the things that matter most in your life: family, friendships, and positive experiences.

IMMEDIATE V. DELAYED GRATIFICATION

Much of your approach to money, your attitude towards it, your habits, are influenced by where you come from and how you grew up. Some people develop money smarts by watching the mistakes of those close to them. This can be a brilliant education.

Eric Wisnefsky grew up in a lower middle class family in central Connecticut. His parents were first generation

Americans and were enamored of wealth and the trappings of success. A new car every three to four years was the norm, whether a new car was needed or not. Debt was created to pay for a lifestyle they could not comfortably afford. Eric was cognizant of all of this in a precarious way and he rejected his parent's love of consumption and financial ways because he saw the stress it created.

Eric was keen to be financially independent. He paid for his college education, additional degrees, and his wedding. He worked full time while in college and delayed getting married in order to save up for the kind of wedding that he and his wife, Tammy, wanted to have.

Unlike his parents, Eric keeps his car until he truly needs a new one.

I tell you this story because one of the most important lessons Eric learned was the difference between immediate and delayed gratification. Impulsively satisfying your immediate needs puts future needs at risk. Financial hygiene and savings is all about delayed gratification.

The concept of delayed gratification was famously studied in the Stanford University marshmallow test in the sixties.[19] During the psychological experiment, Stanford professor Walter Mischel tested four- and five-year-old children on their ability to choose between eating one marshmallow immediately, and receiving two marshmallows if they were willing to wait fifteen minutes. (Note, with delayed gratification you get more, which is a key concept to grasp.)

Mischel followed test participants for years after the study and discovered the participants who exhibited the ability to delay gratification had higher SAT scores, lower Body Mass Index (BMI), and higher educational levels than those students who did not delay gratification.

Although I could not find data supporting the theory that the participants who delayed gratification saved more, there is evidence they earned more—my intuition tells me they saved more, too.

If possible, delay gratification. You'll get more in the long-run.

CREDIT CARDS = IMMEDIATE GRATIFICATION

A few weeks ago, I bumped into a friend who chatted with me about her young adult daughter who had just graduated from college. Living on her own, the daughter was beginning to encounter and understand financial choices and decisions. For example, she was interested in going on vacation with some college friends, and was inclined to charge the proposed trip with a credit card, thus paying for the trip over time. My friend admonished her daughter for thinking along these lines, and encouraged her to instead save up for the trip and pay for it all at once.

If our vacationing friend paid for the $1,000 vacation with a credit card instead of cash, the vacation would cost $1,091, as the interest accumulates until the minimum monthly payments finally satisfies the $1,000 balance due. Maybe the additional $91 doesn't look like a big deal, but it represents a 10 percent tax. When you become desensitized to paying a 10 percent premium, pretty soon you're incurring another $91 here, another $57 there. In no time, you're racking up hundreds of dollars in interest fees.

Let's take a closer look. What would that $1,000 be worth if she delayed gratification; if she chose not to take the vacation at all? Assuming she earns 7 percent on the $1,000 it would be worth $1,967 in ten years; $3,870 in twenty years; $7,612 in thirty years, and a full $14,974 in forty years. Delaying gratification matters and is rewarded.

As a young adult, you cannot delay everything and you'll need to satisfy some present-day desires. Your task is to be aware and understand the implications of delaying or not. Eschewing credit cards to pay for something like a vacation is always wise advice.

WAIT BEFORE YOU BUY

Before deciding to buy something, check yourself by delaying the decision a day, a month, or even a year . . .

If you still feel passionate about the decision after a self-imposed time delay, maybe it is, indeed, the right thing to do.

If your resilience wanes with time, well I guess you really didn't need or want whatever you were contemplating.

Here's a strategy Ann Zipkin has put into place: whenever she wants to purchase something online, she lets it sit in her cart for a few days. If she still thinks she wants or needs it after the self-imposed waiting period, she completes the purchase. What she often finds, however, is that after waiting a few days, she no longer needs or wants the targeted purchase.

Try to force yourself to wait on purchases or major decisions.

A GOOD SALARY DOES NOT GUARANTEE WEALTH

Wealth management professional, Geoff Dietzel, observes that it's not necessarily the type of job or career you have that leads to wealth or independence. (Another reason you should not be too concerned about your beginning compensation when you get your first job.) Geoff sees people with blue-collar, hourly-wage jobs achieve financial independence all the time. Geoff also sees people in executive or professional roles with high annual salaries who can never achieve financial independence.

Geoff attributes this to the fact that you must control spending, save, and invest to attain financial independence. And it's extremely rare that a big salary can overcome unconstrained spending habits.

So take it from Geoff: the single most important concept to learn and internalize in personal finance is the habit of saving. Save, and you will have the highest probability of achieving your financial goals.

EMBRACE FRUGALITY

I encourage you to think about living frugally and modestly. This doesn't mean you shouldn't enjoy life, just be parsimonious with your spending—it can relieve a lot of stress in your life.

There are many creative ways to live, travel, and truly relish life without putting a strain on your spending. For example, we recently went hiking and camping in some western National Parks. It was interesting to see some people roll into a campground in fully tricked out and luxurious recreational vehicles (I'm talking rock star touring buses!) and others, modestly sleeping in tents under the stars. Both choices have positive and negative elements and both choices have implied costs. But, both choices put you in the same beautiful National Park, with the same amazing hiking, and the same stunning views.

So, you can experience something identical with two very different approaches and spending requirements.

BE A SLEEPER, NOT AN EATER

I like to describe money in terms of two bodily functions: eating and sleeping. If you spend a whole bunch, you're an eater; you want to consume—and you might enjoy it very much. If you do not spend, you're a saver and sleep peacefully and easily.

You need to find the right mix and balance for yourself, but a long, good night's sleep is worth a lot.

SAVINGS

You may have inferred this already, but it bears saying: the most important part of your budget should be savings. Growing wealth is not that hard if you start saving as early as possible and do it consistently over very long periods of time.

Time can be your friend or your enemy. If you start saving early, you've enlisted time as a trusted ally. If you mistakenly start savings late in life, time will be an enemy that you will not be able to beat.

Jim Ratliff asserts that from your very first paycheck, and every paycheck thereafter, you should have some portion of your net pay automatically deposited into long-term savings and investments. This is not only financially prudent, but psychologically satisfying too.

THE MAGIC OF COMPOUND INTEREST

The power of starting to save early lies in the growth of your capital through interest, dividends, and capital appreciation. This is the magic of compound interest; where your capital multiplies, as interest earns interest upon itself.

As you continue to add savings, your capital will grow painfully slow, tortoise-like at first; then, as your contributions continue and you enjoy the benefits of compound interest, your savings will begin to rapidly snowball.

Let's consider three savings strategies, which are developed for illustration purposes. In all cases I'm assuming the savings invested in a broad-based portfolio grows at 7 percent per year.

Early Edith starts early and saves and invests $5,000 per year between the ages of twenty and forty, but then terminates her savings program. Late Larry starts late and saves and invests $5,000 per year between forty and seventy, and then stops. Persistent Peter, our most ambitious saver, puts away $5,000 per year between twenty and seventy.

Look at the impact of these three choices:

	Start Age	End Age	Years	Savings/ Year	Total Invested	Growth Rate	Total $ at 70
Early Edith	20	40	20	$5,000	$100,000	7.0%	$1.77m
Late Larry	40	70	30	$5,000	$150,000	7.0%	$0.51m
Persistent Peter	20	70	50	$5,000	$250,000	7.0%	$2.28m

Wow, look at how poorly Late Larry fares. He accumulates $511,286 at age seventy and invested a full $50,000 more than Early Edith, who winds up with $1,771,985 at age seventy. Let's play that back: Late Larry invests 30 percent more money than Early Edith, but only winds up with 28 percent of her accumulated savings.

This highlights the penalty of starting a savings program late and the huge advantage of starting a savings program early.

Again, Early Edith only invests and saves for twenty years, with less money invested than Late Larry, who invests for a full ten years more. Despite these facts, the magic and power of compounding interest works in Early Edith's favor and she builds a sizable nest egg by age seventy; while Late Larry does not enjoy the power of compounding and winds up with far less than Early Edith.

Remember, both earn the same return on their investments, so there's no advantage in the rate of return in either scenario. Because Late Larry waited until he was forty to start his savings program, time became Late Larry's enemy.

Then, there's Persistent Peter, who wisely starts early and keeps on saving and investing until he's seventy—at which time he winds up with $2,283,271 and will retire far more comfortably than either Early Edith or Late Larry.

Persistent Peter enjoys the benefits of starting early and not stopping. This is where the energy of compounding interest really works its power. Please note that Persistent Peter does indeed invest more money than either Early Edith or Late Larry, but look at the result of Persistent Peter's strategy as compared to our other savers.

The punch line here is to save and invest early: that's the single smartest financial decision you can make.

What you invest in matters far less than starting the program at an early age, and contributing to it on a regular basis. *However,* I strongly recommend that you invest in a broadly diversified equity index fund that you can find at Vanguard, Fidelity, or Schwab.

With that, I'll leave you with the often-repeated quote from Albert Einstein: "Compound interest is the eighth wonder of the world. He who understands it, earns it. He who doesn't, pays it."

HOW MUCH TO SAVE?

Think about the example above. Two of our savers accumulate over $1 million by investing $5,000 per year. There's nothing grand or sophisticated about that. I'm not going to say that saving $5,000 a year is easy, but if you want to have something in the future, you must manage your spending to include the ability to save. I'm not advocating saving $5,000 as a specific amount. If you can save more, you absolutely should.

Typically, people earn more as they move through life. If this is the case, resist the temptation to spend all your incremental earnings; save it, instead.

INVESTING: WHAT TO DO WITH YOUR SAVED MONEY

When you think about savings try not to get lost in what exactly to do with the money. The fact that you saved, instead of spent, is the most important step and will put you in a great spot.

I encourage you to use your savings to invest in public securities (stocks and bonds). This is where you'll enjoy the most compounding over time. While leaving your money in a bank account may be more secure, it will not give you the opportunity to grow your savings.

To make progress, it's important that you grow your savings more than the rate of inflation, which I think of as approximately 3 percent over long periods of time. When you're young, you can take risks and have all of your money in equities, rather than bonds. This heavier-on-stocks-lighter-on-bonds approach is definitely riskier, but provides the most opportunity for growth. As you get older, and accumulate savings, it might be more prudent to have some of your money in bonds. You tolerate less risk as you grow older because you don't have as much time to recoup losses.

When you save, it's best to invest your money in broad, well-diversified index funds. This is by far the simplest and cheapest way to allow your savings to grow. Resist the temptation to make concentrated investments in single companies where outcomes can be highly variable. Investing in broad index funds will smooth your ride and position you for the best success. While there are many index funds, I would stick with firms like Vanguard, Schwab, or Fidelity. These organizations provide excellent service and an easy way to invest in index funds. I would choose a single fund that gives you exposure to the total U.S. stock market or the world stock market.

When you save, you will see your account balance move up and down with the ebbs and flows of market performance. Be unemotional. Avoid looking at results and performance too frequently. Let compounding work for you by staying the course. Withdrawing savings in down cycles is just about the worst thing you can do.

It bears mentioning that saving and investing in stocks and bonds is indeed investing, while purchasing homes, cars, watches, furniture is not investing—it's consumption.

DEBT

Debt. This small, single word has brought much pain to many people. Debt is when you owe somebody money. There are several types of debt, but most are awful and should be avoided like a life-threatening disease. Being in debt can be a vicious cycle that envelops your existence and suffocates your happiness.

How do most people get into debt? Simply by spending more than they earn and taking on debt to fill the gap. Avoid this at all costs.

Typically, people accumulate debt by using credit cards and not fully paying the balance each month. Once you start to carry a credit card balance, you must pay the credit card company interest every month. This might sound a bit like compounding interest, which we just discussed, and it is. The only problem is that it's working in the wrong direction: you're providing the credit card company with interest upon interest, and the interest rate charged by credit card companies is typically excessively high. This is a horrible situation that must be avoided.

Use credit cards for convenience (it is simpler than carrying around cash and often comes with helpful purchase protections from the credit card companies), but under no circumstances whatsoever should you carry a credit card balance. If you find yourself in the situation where you can't pay off the balance, it simply means you're spending more money than you can afford.

Credit card companies will tell you that you're only required to pay the monthly minimum balance, or less than you actually charged. Never do that. If you only make the minimum monthly required payment, you will immediately be charged interest and you have slipped into debt.

People often use debt to purchase a home or car, much like Eric's parents did. I would be very careful about both. If you need to purchase a car, use debt sparingly. Every dollar you put into a car is a dollar you're not putting into savings. Fancy and luxurious cars are not an investment. If you purchase a home, you will likely need a mortgage (a fancy word for debt) to do so.

You should carefully scrutinize your budget to make sure you can afford your monthly mortgage payment. Disregard what a bank says you can afford; make that decision independently and for yourself. Trust that you have your own best interest at heart; no one else does. Don't take on too much debt in a home purchase. If you at all feel stressed or uncomfortable, get a more modest house. Please think about a ten- or fifteen-year mortgage, as compared to a thirty-year mortgage. This will require a larger monthly payment, but will help you retire the debt more rapidly, and you will save significantly on interest payments. As an example, if you have a $250,000 mortgage and interest rates are 5 percent on both a fifteen-year loan and a thirty-year loan, you will end up paying $105,857 in interest on the fifteen-year loan and $233,139 on the thirty-year loan. The monthly payment on the fifteen-year loan will be $1,977 and the monthly payment on the thirty-year loan will be $1,342. So, the monthly payment for the thirty-year loan is $635 less, but you pay off the $250,000 loan a full fifteen years earlier and save $127,282 in interest expense. Please note that in my example, I am assuming that the interest rate in both scenarios is identical. In reality, a fifteen-year loan will always have a lower interest rate than a thirty-year loan—implying you will save more.

Debt should be eschewed. If you do take on debt you need to fully understand how it works and how it fits into your budget. The best way to sidestep this is to simply avoid it.

INSURANCE

Unfortunately, bad things can happen in life and one way to mitigate this risk is by having insurance. Insurance allows you to be compensated in situations where you have suffered a loss. Some types of insurance include auto, home, health, and life. There are others too that might be useful as you get older. You should absolutely have auto, home, and health insurance. Without insurance, a loss in any one of these arenas is difficult to recoup.

Sometimes young people see insurance as an unnecessary expense and are willing to take the risk that nothing bad will happen to them. You should think about insurance as having a partner when something unexpected and bad happens in a big way.

As for what coverage to choose, focus on insurance at the high end, not the low end. The difference tends to lie in deductibles—how much money you must pay out of pocket before the insurance company kicks in. The less you pay for your monthly premium, the higher your annual deductible, which means you'll have to pay more for healthcare before the plan kicks in (for example, you can pay $885 a month, with a $5,000 deductible; or $1,700 a month, with a $2,000 deductible).

Health insurance is really important if you need a complex surgery that costs several hundred thousand dollars—this is the design of high-end plans. Health insurance is not that important if you need to visit your doctor because you have the sniffles—this is the design of low-end plans.

Life's unpredictable. Make sure you're covered.

WRAP UP

Be a saver, not a spender. Live within your means. The compounding effect is your best friend, the most reliable builder of wealth—unless you have it turn against you by incurring credit card debt. How you manage your finances is all about choice. Our society is filled with people who seek instant gratification and put off saving and investing. Don't be one of them. When thinking about your finances, simpler and less complex is just about always better. You only need one bank account and one credit card. Your savings plan can be simple and streamlined. Complexity usually means costlier, and more confusion and stress. Insure yourself for loss.

WHERE TO LIVE

The last of the big decisions you'll need to make in life: where to live. One of the big three—next to whom you marry and what you do for work—it tends to make up the foundation of your happiness. Much like the other two, spend a ton of time thinking about this decision. Don't rush. Do everything you possibly can to get it right.

Sarah Bowen Shea, who grew up in Connecticut, agrees; where you live is a huge decision with many implications, which is why you want to pick your place carefully. She chose to live in Portland, Oregon, for a few reasons. She values being outside with temperate weather and beautiful scenery.

She asserts that regions and cities attract certain types of people and you need to know where you'll be happy. Where you are impacts your day-to-day happiness significantly. Every city or town has a culture and you need to get a feel for it to make sure it's a match for you.

Therefore, where you choose to live should be an active

choice. Resist the temptation to default into a decision randomly. As Sarah discovered, where you choose to live will determine many things:

- **Your lifestyle**. For example, if you live in a pedestrian friendly environment, you might be apt to walk more and get more exercise; you might need fewer cars. Something as simple as a pedestrian-friendly setup can have long lasting and compounding health and financial implications. Where we live—suburban Connecticut—is pretty car-centric. This is likely not the case in Boston or a college town like Hanover, New Hampshire.

- **The types of people you interact with**. Communities tend to have cultures and personalities. Some cities or towns orbit around a specific industry that attracts certain types of people. Some towns are very artsy or creative. Some towns lean towards a specific political orientation. Sarah calls this finding your 'tribe', the kind of people with whom you can connect and share time and activities.

- **How much money you spend**. Not only do some locales have a higher, or lower, cost of living, but people tend to behave similarly and mirror norms. So, if you live where people all tend to dine out frequently or take lavish vacations, you cannot help but be influenced by that explicitly or through osmosis. No matter how strong a person you are, you'll be shaped, at least a little, by your environment.

To start, when it comes to finding a place to live, try to target a place where you're about average on a socioeconomic basis. I'm not sure you would like to live somewhere where you feel like you are at the low end of the scale, nor would you want to live at the tippy top of the spectrum.

CHARACTERISTICS TO CONSIDER WHEN CHOOSING A PLACE TO LIVE

- Size of the community
- Proximity to leisure activities you enjoy
- Emphasis on education in the school system and the quality of the school system
- Career prospects
- Presence of creative people
- Focus on arts and culture
- Proximity to an airport—especially a hub airport
- Housing costs and selection
- Community feel—sprawl or high density
- Crime and safety
- Religious mix and openness
- Average age of the population
- Economy—single industry or diverse
- Community activities and events that bring people together
- Vibrancy of the library
- Weather—and its impact on lifestyle
- Activity level of the population—active or sedentary

It might be worthwhile, by the way, to rent an apartment or home in the community you are targeting as a test drive of sorts.

TO BUY OR TO RENT

Once you select the community in which you want to live, you'll need to decide whether to have a house or an apartment, and whether to buy or rent. As always, you just want what's right for you.

Renting will give you more flexibility to move around and change your mind—you won't have to sell something to move along.

Owning a home is ingrained in our psyche and is emotion driven, but it locks you in. Also, the notion that real estate values will always go up is not necessarily true. Owning a home is a highly-concentrated bet on one property, in one community—one that may not hold its value, or worse, suffers a loss.

To help you figure it out on your own, take advantage of interactive online tools, such as the buy vs. rent calculator from *The New York Times*—it can help you think about the financial opportunities of buying versus renting.[20]

SMALL HOME VS. LARGE HOME

If you choose to purchase a home, consider going smaller rather than larger.

Many things are positively correlated with the size of your home: real estate taxes, maintenance, insurance, and the need to accumulate and fill the home—all of which add cost to your life. If your home is smaller, all of these costs tend to be smaller too.

This decision is also part of living within your means. I'll repeat myself here: buying a home is consumption, not investment. Do not delude yourself.

DIFFERENT PLACES FOR DIFFERENT CHAPTERS

Like choosing a career, where you live is not a permanent decision. There are probably appropriate places to live in different chapters of your life: post-college, first married, one child, multiple children, empty nest, and retirement.

Changing the venue, so to speak, can be exciting and positive. Some people periodically move for work, or because they just want to try a new location that might be a better match for them. I actually wish we had lived in a few more places, just to see more parts of the country, or world, and enjoy different perspectives, lifestyles, and experiences. Maybe that will happen yet.

GROWING ROOTS IN ONE SPOT

There's something comforting about living in one spot for a long period of time. You can fully immerse yourself in the community, know the area well, and develop meaningful relationships with neighbors.

Your mom and I have lived in the same general area of Connecticut for about twenty-five years. Obviously, we enjoy it; we're happy and comfortable. I'm not sure I would have selected this area with a blank piece of paper in front of me, but my life unfolded in such a way, what with me starting a business here in 1991, that this is where we began to put down roots and build a life and family.

As you consider where to live, remember growing roots in one spot can be good, too.

WRAP UP

Think of where you live and your home as a backdrop for your family. It sets the stage for so many parts of your life. What kind of people do you want to surround yourself with? What kinds of activities or opportunities do you want easy access to? Which community will best support your priorities and values? Explore the options carefully.

SECTION 2:
WHO ARE YOU?

WHO ARE YOU?

When I was a little boy, it was common for adults to ask, "What do you want to be when you grow up?" My typical reply tended to be fireman, policeman, astronaut, or professional athlete—none of which I remotely had the skill to do. What's interesting about the question is that it's loaded with assumption. It emphasizes a career mindset: you are what you do; your job matters a great deal and defines you as a person.

In comparison, when Jim Smith interacts with his children, who are in their late twenties, and their friends, he likes to ask, "Who are you?"

Can you imagine the vexing frustration in a twenty-seven-year-old when being queried, "Who are you?"

"Who are you?" gets to the essence of how you see yourself—your core and character, what type of person you aspire to be. With no simple or reflexive answer, it's much deeper and more challenging to answer than "What do you want to be?"

Although I led this book off discussing the major decisions that will affect your well-being and success, thinking about who you are is a central theme. If it's at all possible to understand what type of person you want to be and what you want your life to look like, you'll likely achieve more happiness, satisfaction, and fulfillment. If you understand who you are, you'll have a set of values and characteristics that define your life and the decisions you make. Choosing your life-partner, your career, where you live, will be that much easier.

Knowing who you are will be your compass and better ensure you have a life based on character, and filled with purpose.

I'm not necessarily proposing that you mechanically map out every step of your life with laser-like precision. Life has too many wonderful serendipitous twists and turns to take that approach. Your course will change too, but who you are should be fairly steadfast. Of course, your core might morph over time, but it would surprise me if it veered drastically.

Similarly, "What do you want to be" remains a perfectly great question to contemplate, that's why I placed that section where I did—but by emphasizing who you are, you'll discover a better answer.

While you'll seek input and guidance from mentors, teachers, and coaches that will help shape your life and the direction you go, the answer to who you are, ultimately, comes from within.

According to Ken Saxon—friend, fellow entrepreneur, and the founder of *Leading from Within*: "A core to a lot of life is learning to be with yourself."

In other words, you really have to figure out who you are and be happy with that person. There are plenty of stretches in life where you're flying solo, and despite having family and friends, you need to be comfortable being alone with the person you have actively chosen to become.

You can change a lot of things in your life—friends, jobs, where you live—but you cannot escape yourself. Think carefully and consciously about who you are, because you must be true to yourself.

VALUES, GOALS, AND MISSION

Values, goals, and mission are squishy concepts for a young adult to think about, but they matter. They're the building blocks, the vocabulary, if you will, of much of what we're about to discuss. I'm going to spend some time defining them here for several reasons: Most happy, accomplished, and successful people have explicit goals. Most happy, accomplished, and successful people have either implicit or explicit mission and values statements. If you choose to develop values, goals, and a mission, you're more likely to achieve what you want and be fulfilled and happy.

I discovered these tools when I was a bit older than you (though still a young adult) through my readings of Jim Collins, a noted author. Much of what I present here follows Collins' methodology and philosophy.

VALUES

Values are core principles that define who you are. Values likely will not change. Think of them as your compass. If you can define and internalize a handful of values, you can establish a clear sense of what you will and will not do. Life becomes a lot easier when you have clear values; they become your self-defined rules and laws; they guide your behavior.

Let's say one of your values is effort. That means you're committed to always doing your best no matter what. You've established a standard and you will know when you are living up to that value, or not.

Once you define your values, you'll want to think about them regularly. They should become more and more a part of you. They'll make it easier to make decisions: if it's consistent with your values, it's a go; if it conflicts with your values, it's a pass.

MICHAEL WASSERSTEIN VALUES AT AGE TWELVE

1. **Support**. Support is an important value because it uses others to help you. Without support, life might be hard. You need others to help you in anything from a sporting event to a test. Others will pick you up if you are not feeling great and support you. Life can't be completed on your own. You need support.

2. **Friendship**. Friendship is an important value because it involves others around you. Without friends, you may feel left out. Friends are the ones that pick you up if you make a mistake or congratulate you if you do something well. Friends are the ones that you stay with for the rest of your life.

3. **Effort**. Effort is an important value because you must always try your hardest in whatever you are doing. It doesn't matter if you don't like the event, you must still give your best effort. There is no point of doing something if you are not going to try. It is important to never give up. Effort is a good value.

4. **Achievement**. Achievement is an important value because it relates to all other values. You must work to achieve. There is no satisfaction when you know that you did not achieve your greatest capacity. Almost everybody that I know wants to make a difference and achieve. Achievement is a good value.

5. **Work**. Work is an important value because you must work at some times in your life. You can't get through life without working at all. I don't mean

work like a job, I mean putting some effort into things. You won't get anywhere in life without working.

6. **Communication**. Communication is an important value because you must communicate with others throughout your life. If you don't know how to communicate, life will be a struggle.

7. **Cooperation**. Cooperation is an important value because it involves working together to achieve something. Life will give you obstacles that you must beat with others. You must be able to work together with these other people to get around the obstacles. One example of a very smart student who was not able to cooperate happened just a week ago. We had to build a tall tower out of toothpicks and marshmallows. The student decided that he would break away from our group and work on his own. This lack of cooperation will come back to hurt him later in life.

8. **Sportsmanship**. Sportsmanship is a huge value amongst my many values. This particular value happens to be important because it can happen on a positive side or a negative side. Every day you encounter successes and disappointments. If you win or accomplish a goal you must do this graciously. However, if you lose, you don't get down on yourself and think your life is over. You must pick your head up and say, "Okay, maybe next time."

These values are great for the twelve-year-old boy you were when you came up with them; they might have applicability for you as a young adult too.

One of the gifts I asked from you for my fiftieth birthday was to update your values. You kindly indulged me and offered this list:

1. Selflessness (put others above you)

2. Determination

3. Curiosity

4. Openness (to others and new ideas)

5. Humility (probably the most important one on this list)

6. Positivity

7. Respectfulness

You can see that over a five-year period some of your values changed a bit, but directionally the values remain similar and consistent.

VALUES EVOLVE

When Jim Smith was younger, in his early twenties, he was cynical and absorbed with himself—or so he claims. He hadn't yet figured out who he was. As Jim matured and evolved, he gradually became more aware of where he wanted to be and the role leadership and values could play in his life. Jim describes his values as evolutionary. He didn't have an epiphany and pivot, rather he took time to get grounded and develop principles.

Jim's values and the values of Webster Bank, where Jim is CEO, are interchangeable:

The Webster Way®

- We take personal responsibility for meeting our customers' needs.

- We respect the dignity of every individual.

- We earn trust through ethical behavior.

- We give ourselves in the communities we serve.

- We work together to achieve outstanding results.

Interestingly, on the Webster Bank website, where these values are featured, the title of the page is "Who we are."

According to Jim, you need to know who you are at your core, in what you truly believe. These are the concepts that allow you to make decisions based on a values set. They're also the concepts that allow you to be a great leader.

Leadership to Jim is touching people in a positive way and making a constructive difference in whatever he does. In that, he believes you can lead from wherever you are, whatever you do.

Spend some time with Jim and you'll soon realize he lives by these principles. So much so, that it's hard to imagine he was ever cynical. His strong sense of values drives his professional and personal actions. And he uses his leadership position to help others build the strength to be principled and positive, too.

Be ahead of the curve: develop a strong set of positive values—then live and lead by them, much like Jim.

CORE VALUES EXERCISE

A recent article in *The New York Times* highlighted Harvard University's "Reflecting on Your Life" program.[21]

The purpose of the program is to encourage freshmen students to think about what they want their college experience to be like, what their dreams are, where they're headed, and to define their personal core values:

> "In the Core Values Exercise, students are presented with a sheet of paper with about twenty-five words on it. The words include 'dignity,' 'love,' 'fame,' 'family,' 'excellence,' 'wealth' and 'wisdom'. They are

told to circle the five words that best describe their core values. The authors then ask, 'How might you deal with a situation where your core values come into conflict with one another?' Apparently, students find this question particularly difficult. One student brought up his own personal dilemma: he wants to be a surgeon, and he also wants to have a large family. So his core values included the words 'useful' and 'family.' He said he worries a lot whether he could be a successful surgeon while also being a devoted father. Students couldn't stop talking about this example, as many saw themselves facing a similar challenge."[22]

It's interesting that one of the premier universities in the country encourages its young freshmen to identify core values and think about how these values will impact their life decisions. But it makes sense. As I've said before, values can act like a compass and will define your character and behavior. If you have tightly defined values, you will immediately know how you will behave in certain situations because it will either be consistent with or in opposition to your values. Sort of makes life easy.

GOALS

Goals are short-term objectives with a defined success or failure. For example, you might have a goal to read one book per month. You know if you have accomplished that goal at the end of each month, or not.

I think goals and objectives are great tools to stay on track and help you move toward what you want. They should link to your values. For example, if one of your values is to be a healthy person, a goal might be to exercise five times per week.

And don't underestimate smaller goals, intermediate milestones that help you navigate the process in a deliberate and controlled way. Sometimes it's hard to stay focused on a big goal without those baby-step wins.

You might write your goals down. Writing them down makes them more real, a stronger commitment. Then find easy ways to measure progress or completion—a grownup version of the sticker chart used to get you to brush your teeth when you were little.

I don't recommend having too many concurrent goals. Around five goals at any one time would be enough. The good thing about goals is they can change; when you accomplish one goal, you can mark it off your list, and add another.

MISSION STATEMENT

A mission statement is defined as a formal summary of the aims and values of a company, organization, or individual. It outlines a general purpose, something you're trying to achieve or create. While a goal can be short-term or achieved, a mission statement is more of an overarching purpose.

When it comes to mission statements, they should be succinctly summed up. My mission: I am "focused on being a good husband, a good father, and a good friend." My orientation is clearly around those relationships that matter most to me; that's the center of my life. I am clear that my priority is my family and close friendships. I might have other goals in my life that are experiential or bucket list type concepts, but my driving force is to invest in, nurture, and enjoy those relationships that I believe are permanent, are lifelong, and matter most. I want to allocate my time—the greatest indicator and manifestation of what you care about and value—to my family and friends. I want to be physically, mentally, and emotionally available for those I love.

If you can define a mission for yourself, that would be a fantastic accomplishment. It could help you laser in on what you and your life are all about; what you're dedicated to and focused on. If you have something like that in place you can stay on a path and resist distraction and the temptation to deviate from your mission.

WRAP UP

If you have tightly defined values, you will immediately know how you will behave in certain situations, because it will either be consistent with or in opposition to your values. If you look at values individually, they have meaning and significance. But if you bring values together and live those values consistently, that's character and who you are. If you have specific tangible goals, you are more likely to stay on track. And a mission can serve as a filter of sorts when you are deciding if an activity or endeavor is the best use of your limited time and energy.

CHARACTER AND VIRTUES

If values are the goal, virtues are the way to get there. Think of them as the building blocks that lead to character. Virtues are innate, good qualities or morals within people.

Many great thinkers, both ancient and modern, have contemplated how virtues play into character . . .

Plato defined four cardinal virtues as prudence, justice, temperance, and courage.

Aristotle, Plato's student, wrote about and defined virtues and vices, defined the ideal balance point as the *golden mean*— that midpoint of equilibrium that shuns excessive extremes.

Ben Franklin—author, inventor, scientist, entrepreneur, statesman, America's own Renaissance man—defined thirteen virtues and a system to help him embrace and internalize those virtues in order to develop his character.

Character is the foundation for happiness and success in life: how you think about who you are; how you think about how you'll act and behave. We'll start with a few basics, small innocuous things you may overlook because they're so fundamental, but will make a big difference once you start your independent life.

DO WHAT YOU SAY YOU'RE GOING TO DO

Do what you say you're going to do. Sometimes it amazes me just how low the bar is to stand out. Many people over promise and under deliver. They miss deadlines and fall short. You can stand out in many areas of your life, personal and professional, just by doing what you say you will do.

If you tell a friend you will help him out with a project on Saturday at 11:00 a.m., show up on time and ready to help. If a paper is due in your history class on Thursday at 2:00 p.m., get it in by that time. If your credit card needs to be paid in full by the end of the month, set it up for auto payment or make sure you submit it on time.

People tend to model behaviors. If you demonstrate doing what you say you'll do, people in your life will likely reflect that back to you. Additionally, once you establish a pattern of doing what you say you will do, people begin to respect your word and place a lot of trust and faith in you. You build up goodwill; people will be forgiving on the rare occasion when you have a miss—and everybody periodically has a miss.

Conversely, if you're a person who is always late, misses the mark, or doesn't deliver, you develop a bad reputation that is hard to overcome.

Not to mention, it's usually easier to do what you promise rather than have to come up with lame excuses for why you failed.

GOOD MANNERS GO A LONG WAY

Develop and use good manners. As you shift into young adulthood, manners matter more in academic, social, and business settings. I have never seen someone say, "He's a bad guy (or gal)

because he's polite and has good manners." Not once.

Look people in the eye when you talk to them, give them a deliberate and firm handshake, say their name when you greet them, actively listen when they speak and always thank people. This will serve you well in many arenas.

TREAT SERVERS WELL

Something I always try to observe in other people is the manner they use with people who are serving them: how they treat a waiter or a waitress in a restaurant, a clerk in a store.

I've been in the uncomfortable position of witnessing unnecessary rudeness and a lack of appreciation from others. I remember once being with someone in a restaurant, who constantly berated our server. Nothing could please my dinner partner. I thought the service and food were perfectly fine, but my friend could not be satisfied no matter what. My friend was rude and condescending and I thought less of him by the end of the meal.

Thankfully, I've also witnessed people treat those serving them with dignity, appreciation, and respect (mysteriously, it usually results in better service, too).

When you're in a situation where somebody is serving you, be especially polite and appreciative. It's the right thing to do and will show your inner kindness.

ON THAT NOTE, BE FRIENDLY TO EVERYBODY

When you were little, I would drive you to school every morning and bludgeon you with my quotidian advice:

> Try your hardest; pay attention; and be nice to everybody, especially the kid that most needs a friend.

Still applies today.

Befriending "the kid" that needs it most does not change as you get older. You will witness people in college, at work—through middle age and beyond—who need a friend. I'm not espousing that you be best friends with everybody; but be kind and be friendly to everybody, especially to those people who most need a friend.

Examples of this might include inviting someone whom normally might eat alone to eat lunch with you, or asking a new neighbor to join you on a bike ride as a welcoming gesture to the community.

You, too, will be in situations where you are the new person, or you just feel a bit out of place. Think how much you would appreciate a kind smile or someone talking to you, or including you in a conversation or gathering. You might also note this around certain holidays when people do not have a place to go. It's a thoughtful gesture to include that person; and while it may seem insignificant to you, it will no doubt be thoroughly appreciated and remembered by the recipient.

BEWARE THOSE WHO HAVE NOTHING TO LOSE

Be friendly to everybody, but also recognize that it's wise to be wary of certain people you come across, particularly those who appear to have little to lose. Don't get into a confrontation with this sort. You'll be surprised how people can act if they perceive there's no downside to their actions.

As Bob Dylan once sang, "When you ain't got nothing, you got nothing to lose." If a person is in a difficult place, they have nothing to consider and protect and that can make them very aggressive and threatening. It is paradoxical to think that a person with little can be much more frightening than a person with a lot, but the person with much, has much to lose and consider before doing something foolish. Be wary of someone who appears to have little to lose.

SEND HANDWRITTEN NOTES

Be a handwritten note person. When you thank someone, keep in touch, or recognize someone with a handwritten note, it's thoughtful and special. This is especially true in an age of electronic communication where emails get lost in the medium. It's rare that people communicate in personal correspondence; when you do, it stands out.

When you were in middle school, and won the Memorial Middle School PTO award, I encouraged you to send a handwritten note to the committee for the $50 gift certificate you received. Chris Southerland, the head of the Memorial Middle School PTO committee, was so shocked and touched by your note that he sent you a thank you note for your thank you note. Chris pointed out that writing a handwritten thank you note is a dying art, but one of those things in life with no downside and usually appreciated by the recipient. Chris also recognized your manners and thoughtfulness.

Jotting out handwritten notes is a nice habit to get into and people always appreciate it. In an era of throwaway email communication, it will also make you stand out.

DON'T CURSE

Don't curse, if at all possible. I know that periodically it's bound to happen, perhaps with a group of friends or in the heat of a game—but try to keep it to a minimum, or eliminate it completely. I sometimes curse too much, and always regret it.

Cursing does not reflect well upon you and makes it appear as if you're not in control.

BE A LIFELONG LEARNER

Many people stop learning once they finish school. They consider the active learning part of their development completed. Yet, there are so many wonderful things to discover and explore in life. Try to always have a passion or area of exploration in which you can immerse yourself.

Reading is a convenient and easy way to learn about new areas. Will Thorndike, author of the fantastic book *The Outsiders*, emphasizes the importance of reading. Cultivating the habit of being an avid and voracious reader helps you learn and develop a broad perspective.

Read books on topics outside of your direct area of interest and comfort zone. This will help you expand your horizons and understand new topics and points of view. I tend to read too much non-fiction, but you can learn just as much through fiction.

Try to read daily. Some of the people I spoke with during this project told me they have a goal of reading one book per month. You cannot read too much.

Be a lifelong learner with a deep intellectual curiosity. As you age, don't be scared to learn a new language or an instrument. Learning will introduce you to new concepts and people. It will keep you fresh and sharp. Once you stop learning, you quickly begin to atrophy.

PUSH YOURSELF TO BE ACTIVE

Don't stop being active, no matter what.

It may be hard for you to comprehend, but at some point your physical abilities will start to attenuate. I know people my age who no longer run, ski, bike, or play tennis. Sometimes it's due to a bad knee or back or being overweight.

Push yourself to stay physically engaged in activities at all stages of your life. The best way to *stay* active is to never stop being active.

VALUE EXPERIENCES MORE THAN THINGS

People and experiences tend to be more meaningful than objects and things. So try to use your time and money to collect experiences that will bring you joy and positive memories. (Take lots of pictures!)

Focus on those who matter to you and use your resources to engage with those people.

Things tend to be burdensome in the long run. Houses, boats, cars, and other physical objects require maintenance and expense. And oftentimes, things that were initially thought of as objects of joy become masters of your time and money.

I have witnessed boat owners who are enthusiastic about their maritime purchase only to discover the cost and work of owning and maintaining a boat are far more burdensome than they bargained for. Over time they tend to use the boat less and are often happy to dispose of it after several years. I also know boat owners who are passionate about their hobby and use the boat frequently—especially as a vehicle to bring family and friends together. (I often joke with friends who have these toys that I'm an excellent guest: I arrive on time; help as much as I can; complement your kids and wife; bring lavish gifts; and send prompt, flattering thank you notes when I depart. I say this teasingly, but I would much rather be the guest than the host.)

Try to fill your life with people who are important to you and experiences that are fun and broadening. Stuff can create more responsibility, clutter, and stress.

EMBRACE SIMPLICITY

Keep it simple. You heard me say this in regards to your finances. All areas of life tend to be much easier when things are simple.

My dad has often said to me that if you don't have electric

windows in your car, your electric windows will never break. Sometimes people complicate their lives with complexity and that creates more stress and problems. Nobody ever says I want to make my life more complicated. Usually what happens is you think by doing something, you'll experience more joy and pleasure. In reality, when you do that thing, you really create more anxiety, work, and entanglements.

More often than not, simple usually is superior to complex in just about all parts of your life.

Smaller homes are easier to maintain and take care of than bigger homes. One home is easier to administer than two homes. Just to give you two examples.

I have plenty of friends with large homes and multiple homes. And I fully understand why they landed where they did; because at first blush you think more is better and bigger is better.

I have foolishly made many decisions and mistakes that have added complexity to my life, so I'm certainly not immune. To start, I've built three homes, which was actually a process I found very fulfilling, creative, and interesting—but I wouldn't do it again. There are too many easier choices to make.

There's a whole school of thought now that simpler is better and less is more. This is popular and many people have embraced the concept of decluttering their lives by shedding possessions and letting go of all of the 'things' that sap time and energy. The best way to practice this is by limiting the number of things that enter your life in the first place.

My friend Warren Adams is smart, likable, and ambitious. After Warren made his mark in business, he constructed a stunning home of great scale on Martha's Vineyard, Massachusetts. It was truly amazing. Initially, Warren loved the construction process and the forum the house provided for family and friends to convene (or spend time together). But with time, his enthusiasm waned and he grew tired of the mental and physical expense of maintaining the property. I distinctly remember one conversation where Warren said, "I have a vegetable garden the size of a tennis court. I am either weeding and tending to it myself, or paying someone else to do it for me. I can't seem to do anything on a small scale."

Warren loved the great outdoors and in particular fishing. He fell in love with Patagonia, Chile while on holiday there. Instead of just returning there to fly-fish, hike, and horseback ride whenever he wanted, Warren started a for-profit conservation fund investing millions of his own money and acquiring nearly 100,000 acres of land. In the end, Warren's hobby became an all-consuming business venture that took most of Warren's vitality over the past decade.

"In retrospect," he explains, "I often wonder why I had to buy up land and start a business instead of just hopping on a plane and enjoying Patagonia." I don't judge or pity Warren; I do sympathize with him, though. He's like many people who over accumulate and create great complexity where it's not needed.

Ultimately, Warren sold his beloved house and wrapped up his South American business. He now lives in a comfortable apartment in a beautiful city. He goes to Patagonia several times each year for pure enjoyment. And he appears as happy as I have seen him in years.

Of course, we all make decisions in different moments of our lives that would be changed with time and perspective. I see this in Warren and me. The lesson is to be aware of what life chapter you're in and what your specific needs are.

WRAP UP

Character is the foundation for happiness and success in life. I've touched on just a few virtues that will serve you well, that will strengthen your character, but I'd like to dig deeper with a few more.

BE HONEST

Honesty can affect the quality of your life more than any other virtue.

It seems simple and trite to suggest that you should embrace honesty. Being honest has many shades and nuances. But one thing that I'm fairly certain about is this: being honest simplifies your life (a theme you may have noticed by now)—if for no other reason than you don't have to keep track of various truths, half-truths, and lies. It is also inherently the right thing to do.

The dictionary defines honesty as not lying, stealing, or cheating; showing or suggesting a good and truthful character, and not hiding the truth about someone or something: not meant to deceive someone.

I emphasize this with you because many very smart and accomplished people make bad choices at points and appear to drift away from being honest. It's worth thinking about and discussing and internalizing as one of your values.

THE HONOR CODE

I love that at your high school, with every paper you submit, you attest that "I pledge my honor that I have neither given nor received aid on this paper or examination." The Honor Code at your school emphasizes that your word is your bond. The preamble to the full honor code is:

> This we believe: that Personal Honor in word and deed, Personal Integrity in thought and action, Honesty in every facet of life, and Respect for other people and their rights are the essence of a Student of the Taft School.

The U.S. Military Academy raises the bar in its honor code: "A cadet will not lie, cheat, steal, or tolerate those who do." Not only is it wrong to lie, cheat, or steal, but additionally it's a violation to accept and tolerate those who do.

Your honor code is all about being honest in every way.

I suspect at first many people embrace the honor code and being honest at your school because they abhor the consequences of transgression. Suspension, expulsion, notation on a transcript—they're all ways to motivate with the stick.

But I also suspect that students in your high school community appreciate being treated as adults and trusted to act in a way that assumes honesty. It's nice to live in a way that you can trust your peers and exist in a culture and environment that consciously emphasizes honesty and integrity.

Most importantly, you will feel good about yourself by being honest.

BEING HONEST IS EASIER

When I asked Brad Hutensky what he thought was the most important advice he'd been given as a young adult, he didn't blink: *ethical behavior.*

It's easier to be honest because you only have to remember one story and can avoid the complexity of multiple iterations. Also, you only have one reputation and damaging that reputation can be painful, costly, and laborious to repair.

Avoid the grey areas of life. Stay clear of the murky areas where you, or other people, start to feel uncomfortable or your behavior is slipping away from honesty. Act in a way that is honest, even when you are certain you can get away with something illicit. It's one thing to behave honestly when you fear getting caught or consequences; it's another when you have no fear of being discovered and you still act in an honest and pure way.

A constructive way to think about your behavior would be to use Brad's filter: if everybody you cared about were watching you do or say something, would you still be OK with your words or actions? If you feel comfortable doing something or saying something with a hypothetical audience, you're probably on the right track. If you feel squeamish about a peer, friend, mentor, coach, or parent seeing or hearing something, you're probably off track.

Brad is a real estate investor and has multiple institutional investors as partners. He once discovered a situation in his company that made him feel very uncomfortable. In a transaction, something was accounted for as leasing fees, which benefited Brad and his firm more. In reality, the transaction should have been accounted for as a sale transaction.

A year after discovering this accounting glitch, Brad immediately distributed checks to his investors for over $100,000 to account for the discrepancy, reflecting his honest behavior. Brad could have easily kept the $100,000 without anybody realizing the account treatment misclassification, but he did the right thing, even when people were not watching.

Of course, when I asked Brad if he fails and makes mistakes, he chuckled and replied, "Daily."

It's one thing to say you value honesty; it's another thing

to live it. Not being honest can leave you feeling hollow and empty and thinking less of yourself. There are often consequences associated with not being honest, the most important being that you begin to lose your way and veer off the course you want to be on.

POLITE FABRICATIONS

Honesty has degrees of gradation. We all, including me, engage in polite fabrications to make a situation palatable. For example, is it dishonest to respond to your host that you love the dessert when you truthfully do not? I'm not sure this is an ethical transgression that mars you character.

One way to think about a situation like this is whether the misdirected reply would cause unnecessary pain and whether that pain is greater than the fabrication.

Compare the above example to cheating on a test, embezzling funds, or outright lying about your activities when asked by a parent or teacher. These examples clearly feel wrong and there is no benefit, other than your personal gain.

ADMIT YOUR MISTAKES

At times, you'll make mistakes; that's normal and part of becoming and being an adult. When you do, it's best (and easiest) to admit your mistakes and endure the consequences. Not being honest about your mistakes compounds the situation and makes you and other people think less of you.

Last year, a friend's son, Tad, made a pretty big mistake in my mind. He was at a friend's house and made a foolish decision to have alcohol with a group of friends. I don't know if Tad felt peer pressure to participate in a bad decision, or if he consciously made a bad choice independently. Either way, it was not his best moment.

Despite the unfortunate situation, one thing I do respect

and appreciate about Tad was the fact that he told his parents the truth. Tad was still punished; and his parents did a lot of talking about poor decisions and alcohol, but they were glad he told them what happened. If Tad had decided to be dishonest, he would have made a bad situation far worse, and his parents would have been in the bad place of having their trust level for Tad diminished.

Your reputation and integrity is based on your actions and honesty. In most situations, you're given the benefit of the doubt and people assume you are authentic and display veracity until you do not. Unfortunately, once you violate someone's trust it can be extraordinarily difficult, or impossible, to earn back.

WHEN YOU LOSE YOUR MORAL COMPASS

Although being honest seems obvious, people at all levels of education, success, and power seem to veer off course at times. Nobody appears to be immune.

Eugene Soltes, a professor at Harvard Business School, wrote the book *Why They Do It: Inside the Mind of White Collar Crime*, which explores how and why people who clearly know right from wrong lose their moral compass and behave dishonestly and illegally. Generally, people lose their way incrementally, without grand malicious initial intentions. Then things snowball.

Soltes asserts that part of the problem in misbehavior is the perceived distance and lack of connection between victims and those committing crimes. It feels very different to march into a bank and demand money with a gun pointed at a nervous teller than for an executive to misappropriate funds from anonymous people. The outcomes might be similar, but we view the crimes very differently. Similarly, you can rationalize cheating on a test by telling yourself no one will get hurt, that there is no victim.

Of course, the victim in all cases is the person who violated their own honesty code by lying, cheating, or committing a crime.

ABOVE THE LAW

People sometimes feel above the law or ethics when they achieve a certain level of success. Some people lose their course when in positions of power.

Let me cite an example: President Bill Clinton was impeached in December 1998 for perjury and obstruction of justice in connection with his affair with then White House intern Monica Lewinsky. It's hard to think of a more powerful person than the president of the United States. With that heady power probably comes some feelings of invincibility or a sense of being able to do whatever you want. This, of course, is not true. We're all subject to laws and ethical standards, regardless of our achievements.

Although Clinton was acquitted in the impeachment process in February 1999, he created an awful situation for himself, his family, and our country.

Clearly, Clinton is human and flawed, like all of us, in his ethical behavior.

Please do not forget that wherever you land, whatever you achieve, you're subject to rules, laws, norms, customs, and—most importantly—your own honor code.

WRAP UP

Presidents, successful business people, average Joes, they can all lie, cheat, and steal. No one is immune.

As *The New York Times* columnist Charles Blow once wrote (when discussing the 2016 presidential election), "Presidents lie. Politicians lie. People lie."[23] I, too, have lied and done things that have been dishonest, things I completely regret.

The best course of action is to adhere to your values, ethics, and the laws. Don't lose your way. Once you travel off course, it can be very difficult to recover.

Do your best not to lie or be dishonest. The greatest gift you will receive from that habit is peace of mind and the personal satisfaction of knowing you have not done anything wrong or unethical.

BE OPEN-MINDED AND UNBIASED

From time to time, we're all guilty of approaching people with preconceived notions or judging them on scant information. Perhaps when you first encounter a person, you have an initial reaction based on age, gender, physicality, or clothing. Try to resist this. People are obviously deeper and more complex than a few demographic characteristics or their wardrobe. Try to encounter and engage with people based on their human composition: who they are, rather than what they do or how they appear.

Try to have an open mind—think blank piece of paper— when you first meet someone, especially if they're different from you. You can form an opinion over time after multiple interactions and conversations.

People continually surprise me, both positively and negatively. Sometimes, those I expect to be kind, attentive, thoughtful, and nice are not, and those I mistakenly expect to be brusque, uninformed, and rude are super people. I think this is particularly true when you interact with a person one-on-one and not in a group setting. This oftentimes gives the person an opportunity to reveal his true self instead of playing to a group.

Unfortunately, we're all burdened with our own biases. The key is to try and check yourself and squash any biases you have developed.

Let me try to share a handful of situations, how you can open up your mindset and perceive people for who they really are, not who you suppose them to be at first blush.

VERY SUCCESFUL PEOPLE CAN SOMETIMES SURPRISE YOU

Recently, I visited a couple in Florida whom I do not often see and do not know all that well. They're highly educated, both with advanced degrees; they're well-traveled and well-read; they're cultured and live in a posh location. So imagine my shock when, during our conversation, both made several overtly racist comments that not only made me uncomfortable, but made me think less of them.

I mistakenly expected this couple to behave and think in a different manner based on their high educational background, apparent sophistication, and career success. Anybody can say distasteful things, but I was caught off guard because I absolutely did not expect it.

Sometimes people, including me, mistakenly attribute certain characteristics to very successful, wealthy, or well-known people. They assume they're smart, or always right about everything. I'm sure this is not true for everybody, but I certainly have found myself under the spell of success or fame.

This is because our society places a higher value on achievement than on character. (I've devoted a whole chapter to this concept.)

In reality, people who have achieved a high degree of career or economic success have been at least a little lucky; they might have expertise in one area, but that might not translate to other arenas.

BEING FAMOUS, SUCCESFUL OR WEALTHY DOES NOT MAKE YOU RIGHT OR BETTER

A challenge with being successful is that people constantly reaffirm your success and you can begin to develop hubris.

Let's consider the sad example of famed baseball pitcher Curt Schilling. Schilling was a prolific pitcher—a true success. He led four different teams to the World Series and won three championships. He was a Major League Baseball All-Star no less than six times and a World Series Most Valuable Player once in his twenty-year career. Schilling was unequivocally a successful athlete.

After retiring from baseball, Schilling founded 38 Studios, a company engaged in the business of developing advanced and complex computer games. The company received a $75 million loan from the State of Rhode Island as an incentive to relocate from Massachusetts to Rhode Island. After approximately six years of operations, 38 Studios declared bankruptcy. On a Boston radio station, Schilling admitted to personally losing his entire $50 million fortune.

This is a gloomy story and I share it to highlight that successful people, wealthy people, celebrities are not always right. They are, indeed, fallible. While Schilling was irrefutably successful as a baseball pitcher, he was flawed as a businessperson.

So, while accomplished people can certainly be worthy of emulating or modeling in their specific area of expertise, and even in other arenas, do not assume success in one context transfers to another. Be curious, be polite, but have a healthy dash of skepticism.

In the words of Royce Yudkoff, "Being rich does not make you better than others."

BEING UNSOPHISTICATED DOES NOT MAKE YOU LESS

Going in the other direction, you might encounter people who initially strike you as ill-informed, unsophisticated, or even dim—which may not be the case at all.

Perhaps this person has not enjoyed all of the benefits of a formal education; maybe he didn't have the breaks and advantages you (and others) have enjoyed. Maybe he's just been unlucky, or chose a different life path. This does not mean that person cannot teach you something or be a friend.

When I studied in the Soviet Union as a college student, on more than one occasion I recall jumping into a taxicab and not giving much thought about the person who was ferrying me to my destination. As often happens in those situations, a conversation was struck up, and once the taxi driver realized I was from the United States I was peppered with many curious questions, including my favorite poet.

Truthfully, I did not expect to be quizzed on my favorite poet by the taxi driver; on that day, he was obviously the teacher, and I was the student. I received an informative discourse on Russian poets and a valuable lesson: keep an open mind and drop any preconceived notions. My taxi driver was far more knowledgeable about literary culture than I was.

LEARN FROM EVERYBODY

After Jill Hutensky graduated from the Yale School of Management, she took a job in a management training program at Hartford-based United Technologies. One of Jill's early assignments was to work on the assembly floor at Pratt & Whitney, a United Technologies division. At the time, Jill was a twenty-four-year-old, managing a group of eighteen middle-aged men she originally perceived as less educated laborers.

Jill quickly realized that the people she was managing

knew far more than she did about the technical manufacturing process, which she was leading and overseeing. The experience taught her that whenever you approach people, you cannot go in thinking you're better or know more than someone else. You must understand your place in the situation, what you have to offer, what other people can offer as well. You have to understand that you can learn from everybody and be respectful of people doing the best they can.

TREAT PEOPLE WITH DIGNITY

Bob Galvin, CFO at Holtec, believes all people deserve respect and to be treated with dignity regardless of race, religion, sexual orientation, status level, or gender. He asserts that all people, regardless of their position in life, have character and dignity. Bob does not tolerate people who belittle others based on anything except a lack of character and integrity.

It's especially gracious and kind to go out of your way to be appreciative of and respectful to those people who might not have enjoyed the education, good fortune, or advantages you have had. Bob makes a conscious effort to talk with and demonstrate appreciation to those people who might be first generation Americans and are just starting the American journey and are not as lucky as he has been.

I hope such a mindset would be natural to you.

PEOPLE CHANGE OVER TIME

People also change and develop over time. Sometimes, when a person is young, you think of them in one context; when she grows and matures, she becomes someone else entirely. Think of the neighbor kid who cuts your lawn. In a blink of an eye, that kid is now your orthopedist. In that situation, you cannot think of the fifteen-year-old cutting your lawn anymore, you have to open your eyes and see a talented and educated doctor—who is taking care of you!

I'm inclined to cling to my memory of you as a little boy who begged me to play catch and was dependent on me. But now, within a very short period of time, I see a mature, smart, and caring young adult who's a lot closer to complete independence. That requires a shift in mindset.

DIFFERENT SHOULD BE SOUGHT OUT

One way you can try to learn from people and get practice at not judging others is to intentionally interact and befriend those people who are different than you.

Several decades ago, you could live an isolated life where you only encountered people who were very similar to yourself. Thankfully, that is no longer the case. It's now necessary to have the skills to converse with and leverage different people and cultures.

Willy MacMullen, the headmaster of the Taft School, asserts that difference is not only good, but should be sought out, without judgment, with the desire to understand. Willy acknowledges this is difficult because we all seek and embrace comfort and familiarity. To discover and encounter the different, we need to expend effort and intentionality. He believes that interacting with people who are not like you is incredibly important in life and when doing so you should have an open mind and an orientation towards acceptance.

By wading into the diverse, Willy proposes, you make life more rich and satisfying.

To be a leader today, you must be able to interact with diverse groups of people. Think of your young adult interactions with different types of people as a form of rehearsal and practice to that end.

WALK A MILE IN ANOTHER MAN'S SHOES

In Harper Lee's *To Kill A Mockingbird*, protagonist Atticus Finch embraces the concept of not judging people by saying, "You never really understand a person until you consider things from his point of view . . . until you climb into his skin and walk around in it."

Try to take the other person's perspective when you are tempted to judge someone. The other person is likely doing something similar to what you would do if you were in his or her skin.

Listen to ideas that make you uncomfortable; have empathy to walk in someone else's shoes. You will learn that people view the world in many ways.

IT'S ALL IN THE CONTEXT

Part of who you are depends on context: where and when you were born, how you grew up, and in what circumstances. Some people are fortunate to have lots of good things going for them; some people get an awful hand in life. These situational dynamics shape a person.

You should not be envious of people who have had a better start and situation than you. Nor should you look down on those who have been less fortunate than you. It's all luck.

Sometimes I interact with friends who disparage people who have not been as lucky as they have been. My friends think that those who are not as fortunate or as accomplished are lazy, that they don't work as hard, maybe even that they're taking advantage of certain systems.

But people in different contexts have very different starts in life.

You were nurtured in the womb: Mom took supplemental vitamins, read to you, and played you music; she exercised throughout pregnancy, ate in a healthy way, and went to the doctor regularly to make sure everything was on track in the pregnancy. Consider the day you were born at Waterbury Hospital. You went home to a two-parent family; to a home filled with books, healthy foods, and every imaginable baby toy and device to help develop you in every way. As you got older, it was *Mommy and Me* classes, tumbling, swimming, Spanish for tots, preschool, and more.

In other words, you started in a pretty good place and your context was a fortunate one.

I recall a teenage mother giving birth on the same day you were born, in the same hospital. She was screaming and frantic. The nurses told me the father was not present and she was unmarried. The baby was probably not going home to the same environment you did. Were there books, music, organic food, and classes and lessons of all types? I don't know, but you probably get the point that your context and the baby born to the single, teenage mother in the next room, on the same day, were very different. I will assume that the mother was a caring and loving person and did everything possible for her child, but that child still had a harder start than you.

WRAP UP

Most people have an interesting story and perspective and you can learn something from just about everybody. The key is to make yourself available, to learn, and to be open.

When you meet a new person, consciously try not to pigeonhole that person before you have a real opportunity to understand who they are as a person and learn from them. More often than not, people will pleasantly surprise you if you just give them a chance.

Take care to be kind, be open-minded with people who are different than you, who have walked a different road than you or started from a different place. Such situations can often be the most enlightening and broadening.

DEVELOP GRIT

Grit is such a neat word and encompasses incredibly attractive traits. It may even be the most admirable virtue to possess.

When I was building my first company, I was convinced there were plenty of people who were smarter than me in the industry—plenty of people who had been in the industry far longer than me. What I had was an overwhelming desire to build something special and create my vision of an excellent company. Nothing was going to stop me unless it was illegal or unethical. I was going to run the endless marathon no matter how tired I got, how hard it was, or how many obstacles popped up in front of me.

Of course, there were times I was, indeed, tired; and there were obstacles aplenty. This will be the case for you as well. The defining characteristic—the thing that makes a difference—is grit and an unrelenting desire to make it work.

Those who embrace grit might have a big end goal in mind but they're not scared of the thousands of steps that need to be taken to get there. They don't consider these steps overwhelming, just part of the journey.

Angela Duckworth does an excellent job exploring this concept in her recent book titled *Grit*. She highlights the importance of perseverance—the ability to stick to it, coupled with hard work—as being more important and a higher predictor of success and achievement than intelligence and talent.

I agree. People who have the ability to stay with something until it works always amaze me. Their sheer hunger and tenacity help make something a triumph.

As you think about your career and other aspects of your life, think about grit as something to emulate and embrace; rely on grit as your signature trait—above being smart or naturally talented. I've seen many people who are gifted at something squander that talent by being over-reliant upon it. They don't have the perseverance to drive forward and optimize their talent by coupling it with grit. Don't let that be you.

A MISADVENTURE IN ANTARCTICA

Recently, I read a book about Ernest Shackleton, an amazing explorer in the early twentieth century. While Shackleton accomplished several notable feats, he's probably best known for his misadventures in Antarctica.

Endurance, the ship he captained, became trapped in the ice floes during an expedition that sought to cross Antarctica. Shackleton and his crew endured incredible hardship as their ship was locked in ice and ultimately sank. What's most notable about Shackleton is his leadership abilities and his grit.

The *Endurance* story has more challenges and plot twists than a fabricated Hollywood adventure. After the ice floes broke apart, allowing Shackleton and his crew to make their way to Elephant Island, Shackleton launched an unimaginable open boat journey of 720 nautical miles to South Georgia, where whaling stations operated and help and safety could be found. Traveling in an open boat, on the open seas, for this distance was an ambitious and optimistic strategy, despite being the only logical choice.

Shackleton and his skeletal crew successfully made it to South Georgia, but landed on the wrong side of the island, forcing them to cross the island with no equipment, under treacherous conditions and impossible terrain. (No known crossing of South Georgia had ever been made.) Shackleton and his men persisted and triumphed, arriving at the whaling stations on South Georgia.

After reaching safety, Shackleton began the process of reassembling his crew, men who had been left in various parts of South Georgia, Elephant Island, and McMurdo Sound.

Shackleton displayed tremendous grit and persistence in his Antarctic expedition. He encountered repeated setbacks, disappointments, and unimaginable challenges. Despite these obstacles, Shackleton trudged on, teaching us that, with grit, one can overcome the impossible.

THE TWENTY-MILE-A-DAY MARCH

I first encountered the concept of a twenty-mile march in Jim Collins' writings. Collins contrasts the styles and approaches of two explorers, Roald Amundsen and Robert Falcon Scott, racing to the South Pole. Amundsen trounced Scott in the race, and his team lost no lives in the expedition. Scott, on the other hand, not only lost the race, but lost his life—and the lives of five of his team members.

Amundsen's grit made the difference.

He thoughtfully prepared for the grueling expedition and studied, on a first hand basis, the best transportation modes used by indigenous people, which included the use of dogs and skis. In contrast, Scott hastily built his strategy around ponies and motorized sledges. Amundsen provisioned for his journey in a detailed and thoughtful way and assumed the unforeseen, which he planned for accordingly. Scott had fewer provisions and his provisions were cached in difficult places to access.

What I love most about the Amundsen strategy is his twenty-mile-a-day philosophy—what he called "breaking work up into bite size chunks." He stuck to the predetermined distance goal each and every day, regardless of conditions, regardless of his ability to travel further. This allowed for plenty of rest and steady progression. This tortoise-like strategy was in direct contrast to Scott's hare-like philosophy of excessive progress on good days, to the point of exhaustion, and no progress at all on bad days—which, as you know, turned out badly.

Having the self-discipline to tackle a big goal by breaking it down into tortoise-like chunks and resisting the temptation to over accelerate or take off too much time is essential to success. So many things in life are about small, consistent progression. As Scott learned, it's very difficult to make it up when you take off days.

I've lived by my own twenty-mile-a-day marches. Writing this book, for instance, has been a wonderful journey and exercise for me. I've never written a book before (as you may have noticed); I consider myself an OK business writer, but this project was a version of Amundsen's South Pole for me. I prepped a lot; I thought a lot; I got a lot of input from friends and advisors; I tested the idea with people I respect; but most importantly, I wrote two to four pages per day, whether I felt my muse calling or not. I tended to write at the same time of the day, in the same place. Routine and habit have propelled me forward.

I've resisted the temptation to write more than four pages on any given day and tried to avoid taking a day off from writing (although I certainly have). To my surprise, and the surprise of many of my friends, I'm getting pretty close to my South Pole. It sure feels like I'm going to win my race of writing a book that will be, I hope, useful to you.

Grit is an attitude. It's about tenaciously plowing forward. Combine grit with a twenty-mile-march philosophy, and you've got the formula for success.

Whatever you're doing in your life, embrace grit, and figure out what the twenty-mile march means for you. With these two concepts, you'll achieve most of what you desire in a tortoise-like way.

Think about doing those activities you can do every single day to drive you forward towards your goal. Don't let a daunting task overwhelm you, just figure out those bite-sized segments, and move forward.

WHEN THINGS LOOK BLEAK

Joe Smith believes in perseverance. He remembers a plaque in his dad's office, which read, "Don't Let the Bastards Grind You Down." It's a memento from his father, reminding him to stay with things, especially when they look daunting and bleak. This reminder was especially important when he was in his early twenties and just starting to make his way in the world, when he had little confidence and practical knowledge.

When something doesn't work, you need to accept it, get up, and try to do it again and better the next time. You need to have resilience and grit.

According to Danny Rosen—who completed a PhD, a pretty gritty endeavor—it doesn't matter at all how many times you get knocked down, and you will; it only matters how many times you get back up. Danny is a picture of persistence. Not only did he run the marathon of completing a PhD, but he has also shepherded his family through three cancer deaths, a traumatic fire, and he rode the entrepreneurial roller coaster with multiple leadership changes at his startup project. He has persevered through a lot and he keeps getting up.

As Danny will express, you can't always be the smartest person in the room, but you can be the hardest working. That certainly feels like grit.

THE CURSE OF THE NATURAL

When I was in high school the smartest peer I knew was Robert. Robert was off-the-charts brilliant. He played at a completely different level than most people I knew. A natural, Robert was so innately smart he had little need to actually do any academic work. He coasted through high school effortlessly and got into Princeton without much energy.

After Princeton, Robert bounced around a bit and is now a consultant at a well-known, multinational corporation. But it seems he never really fully hit his stride. Perhaps he never had to develop tenacity, grit, because he was so incredibly smart. This is what is known as the curse of the natural.

According to National Basketball Association (NBA) superstar Ray Allen, success, achievement, and accomplishment in the NBA is not the result of God-given talent or some type of magical formula. It's the result of what he refers to as boring old habits and getting your work in every single day, even when nobody is watching.

Sounds a bit like a twenty-mile march.

People with grit are workhorses, whereas some people who are naturals are show ponies—they look great and should be able to produce, but sometimes they don't actually get anything done. When you make people decisions, always look for grit, over everything else.

WRAP UP

When I was a young entrepreneur I constantly sought the secret recipe for success. I wanted that magic formula that certainly existed somewhere. I chatted up everybody I could. I asked endless questions to endless people about their strategies, execution, and structure. I was a sponge and wanted to ferret out that deep secret that must be.

After countless conversations, I came to the realization,

like Allen, like Amundsen, like Shackleton, like everybody else that puts in the hard work, that there are no secrets or magic. It's all about making prudent decisions, having your boring old habits, and working those habits consistently and relentlessly. It's all about grit.

RESUME VS. EULOGY

Who you are—the core of your character—is much more important than what you achieve and accomplish. Yes, your education and your career choice are important; but who you are as a person, how you treat others, should be your true measure of success.

Mom and I have been told by teachers, coaches—even your own peers—that you're incredibly nice, thoughtful, and kind. I'm very proud of this, because it shows how special you are. As a matter of fact, we've often heard, and I am not engaging in hyperbole here, that you are the nicest student a teacher has taught. Being kind, thoughtful, and nice does not appear on a report card, nor is it listed in who scored the most goals in a soccer game. But it's exactly the type of virtue that matters in this world. It goes to the core of who a person is rather than what they've achieved.

David Brooks authored a wonderful column for *The New York Times* titled *The Moral Bucket List*;[24] it contrasts a life focused on resume virtues and a life focused on eulogy virtues. I hope you find the time to read it—or better yet, read the book, *The Road to Character*, on which the column is based.

Brooks explains, "It occurred to me that there were two sets of virtues, the resume virtues and the eulogy virtues. The resume virtues are the skills you bring to the marketplace. The eulogy virtues are the ones that are talked about at your funeral — whether you were kind, brave, honest, or faithful. Were you capable of deep love?"

Resume virtues tend to be centered around yourself; they're focused on measurable achievement and accomplishment, while the eulogy virtues are indicative of who you are and what your character is at the core—they're outward centered. Your eulogy virtues, by the way, are likely the words and concepts you penned in your mission statement and core values. They're the elements of who you are that hopefully correlate with how people view you as a person.

The problem is, just about every single message you receive as a young adult is keyed in on resume virtues: who gets awards at school; what gets lionized in magazines and newspapers; what, as a community, we hold up as success. These tend to be things that are accomplishment oriented. They're about doing and achieving rather than being and character. This is further exacerbated by the deification of celebrities and their sometimes tawdry behavior. No wonder eulogy virtues end up taking a backseat.

Think about what gets celebrated in the media: people who accomplish. It's understandable, because those are easy stories to write. But, there are many anonymous people who are fundamentally good. As Brooks describes, they radiate an inner light—these people often are not as celebrated as those with resume virtues.

Rick Ruback, a professor at Harvard Business School, once shared a tale of a hard-driving investment banker who sadly died prematurely. At his funeral, speakers regaled the mourners with stories of assiduous work and deal-making skills. One anecdote highlighted the fact that the banker once mistakenly packed two left shoes for an important business trip; he trudged through the day of meetings with two left wingtips, still making deals. While I admire this cute story, it seems somehow wrong that a person is remembered by his deal-making skills, rather than his relationships and character.

I hope people remember me for who I am and how I acted rather than what I did and achieved. I'll admit, when I was younger I was very resume virtue oriented. I was on lots of lists for being young and successful and appeared in more than my fair share of newspapers and magazines. As I've matured I more fully relate to and understand what Brooks is describing and do not want my life to be about resume virtues. I want it to be more about eulogy virtues.

You will, of course, have a combination of virtues in your life, and you need to. The trick is to get them in the balance you want and to not let the resume part of your virtues drown out your eulogy virtues.

BE AWARE OF THE ECOSYSTEM IN WHICH YOU EXIST

We touched on this idea in the first chapter: the people you surround yourself with help establish the norms by which you'll live. Because of this, you can easily lose sight of what matters most to you. When everybody is behaving in an odd way, and it's done together in a closed, self-enforcing bubble, it starts to look and feel normal; and that's the moment you might lose your own way. The emphasis on resume virtues is a case in point.

Be careful and aware of the ecosystem in which you exist. If you exist in a resume-soaked environment, like a hard charging industry or community, where people are primarily focused on career advancement, wealth accumulation, and excessive business travel, this can all become the norm. The most intense resume-oriented people advance and often receive accolades, more power, and more money. Who wouldn't want that? Yet, the potential cost of this single-minded drive is so often downplayed. Not seeing your family for a week due to business travel is encouraged; you'll even take on the macho-moniker of "road warrior." To be the one who travels most in a year, who racks up the most air mileage, is a badge of honor, a form of bragging. Even airlines encourage it, with their *status-preferred* privileges for your travel.

I'm not telling you to avoid this environment, but to only be there if you consciously want to be there. Don't wind up in a place by default or by accident. You might actually learn quite a bit by being there, and you might enjoy it. If you do find yourself in an environment like this, just be aware of where you are—and that the signals and messages you're getting are shaping you.

You would do well to put yourself in a setting where both resume and eulogy virtues are valued.

THE SECRET SAUCE

When Mike Erwin, author, entrepreneur, and professor at West Point, attended West Point, he spent a lot of time thinking and learning about character and leadership. He told me the secret sauce at West Point is an intense focus on achievement (resume) and character (eulogy).

Mike's now in a chapter of his life where he's fully oriented around character. He has developed the *Positivity Project*, which is a deep look at character and how it drives leadership.

Mike teaches that there are twenty-four traits that drive your character, which can be divided into six subgroups. Mike defines character as the intersection of your thoughts, your feelings, and your behaviors. Here's a look at what drives character, according to his *Positivity Project*:

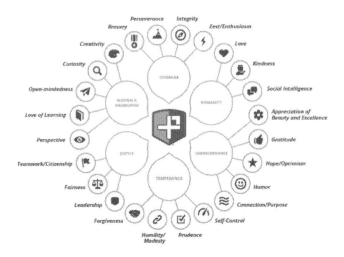

Character drives how we treat other people and our ability to focus on and understand other people. Mike hopes that achievement and relationships stay in balance, but his defining philosophy is focusing on people and relationships

THE RICHEST MAN IN TOWN

It's a Wonderful Life is one of my favorite movies. It may be a bit of a cliché, but it does have a very powerful message and story.

Mr. Potter (our villain, played by Lionel Barrymore) represents resume virtues in that he's all about owning, achievement through possession, and controlling other people. He appears to have few, if any, friends. Portrayed as an insatiable and manipulative accumulator who does not think highly of his fellow citizens, he's not liked by many, and is feared by all.

George Bailey (our protagonist, portrayed by the earnest Jimmy Stewart) is a proxy for eulogy virtues. George is always doing the right thing; even when he thinks he wants to, he cannot do anything selfish.

Throughout the course of the movie, George Bailey discovers what life would be like if he did not exist, without all the positive deeds done in his life. When his angel guide, Clarence, returns him to normal life, George is pleasantly surprised that the entire town gets behind him unconditionally, emotionally, and financially in his time of need. This, in a way, is George's living eulogy—a testament to his character and who he is as a person, constantly sacrificing and giving to other people for the betterment of his community; because it's the right thing to do. George's war hero brother, Harry, gives the culminating line in the film, a toast to George, "the richest man in town."

This clever word selection is obviously in direct contrast to the Potter character, who is economically the undisputed richest person in town. No different than Brooks' resume and eulogy virtues, the Potter and Bailey characters allow the viewer to select who they want to emulate and which model is more important over time.

Of course, Hollywood paints a stark contrast between Potter and Bailey when, in reality, we all possess some resume and eulogy virtue traits. I think these traits can amplify and attenuate in different chapters of life, too.

The important thing for you to think about and figure out is whether you're living your life to build a resume or build a legacy and reputation. If you're not careful and deliberate here, you will likely drift into the direction of resume virtues, because there's so much pull in that direction.

Tom Bird reminds us, "You really need to pay attention to happiness. If you don't, life can sweep you away. If you do not have intentionality in your life, you can wind up somewhere you did not want."

WE NEED MORE GOOD PEOPLE LIKE THIS

A friend shared the story of his father, a young professor in the South, in the late forties. His father and seven other professors, early in their careers, made a bold decision to resign from the university where they were teaching—a very risky move—because the university embraced a policy of explicit segregation, which they found distasteful.

The young professors did not want to compromise their values and perception of what was right, regardless of the consequences. So, they resigned. It sent a strong signal to their university, and to their families.

My friend's dad kept a detailed diary about the situation because he wanted to share this story with my friend; he wanted him to know all aspects and details of what happened.

What a wonderful story and message about character and eulogy virtues, about feeling good about your own moral compass. It was a super decision for my friend's father. The happy twist: he wound up as a professor at Yale and enjoyed a lengthy career there.

THE CATALYST THAT GETS US THINKING

Focusing on eulogy virtues can and will be challenging at times. People and messages that reinforce our resume-virtue society will constantly surround you. Sometimes it takes a big event to get us to think about eulogy virtues. The event can be a dislocation (good or bad), a birth, a death, an illness, or even incredibly good fortune. Whatever it is, we need that catalyst to get us reflecting on where we want to be on the resume-eulogy spectrum.

My first dislocation was selling ArchivesOne, a great event by most standards. This event redirected me from go mode and forced me to pause and reflect and consider my values all over again. I went from every minute of my day being absorbed and scheduled, being the center of everything and "the man," to having more time than I ever thought possible, few phone calls and emails, being forced to abandon the comfort of my prior routine, and needing to decide what was next for me as a person. After selling the business, I was forced to begin anew, and this was really a fantastic opportunity and blessing.

I see so many people who race ahead and never get the benefit of a dislocation. As a result, they never pause and deliberately think about where they want to be or who they want to be. They wake up every day and charge ahead, never really considering the roadmap on which they are relying.

Your uncle Reuben once confessed that when he was in his twenties, he wanted to be famous, wealthy, and have power and prestige. He wanted to do something really important and be successful—to make a notable mark in the world. I appreciate his candid honesty in sharing this. There are probably elements of this in all of us.

As Reuben grew personally, he realized those resume goals were not fulfilling, they weren't a true definition of success. He got dislocated with news of a possibly sick child, which forced him to contemplate his relationships with his children. When a child is potentially sick, priorities quickly change and come into focus.

Reuben reoriented and restructured his life. Through soul searching, he discovered that fame, fortune, and power do not bring fulfillment and happiness. I hope this book helps you think about resume and eulogy before a dislocation. The character virtues and the relationships you have are the true markers of success and happiness.

WRITE YOUR OBITUARY

When Jason Pananos was asked to write his obituary, a form of eulogy, he dutifully complied. This happened while he was still in his twenties, at the behest of a mentor.

When Jason wrote this obituary, he was not on the path to achieving what he wanted. The exercise forced him to consider where he was going and make changes. Jason now believes he's moving in a direction that is closer to what he wants his obituary and eulogy to be.

I, too, once wrote a *pro forma* obituary, six years ago. As I reread the document, it's interesting to see the words I selected, the focus of the text. It was much more about adjectives—who I am—compared to what I did. It centered on relationships with people and exploring, learning and living life in a curious way. It was about my relationship with my wife, my kids, and my grandkids.

I would encourage you to think about writing an obituary for yourself.

THE RELENTLESS PURSUIT OF MORE

In March 2000, *Harvard Business Review* featured a case study entitled *When Everything Isn't Half Enough*.[25] The case study features a fictional protagonist, Norman Spencer, who devotes his thirties and forties to building an investment firm with singular focus. Norman, in his late forties, realizes he's extraordinarily successful and has accumulated all the trappings and earmarks of achievement, and resume virtues: multiple palatial homes, awards, boards of directorships, and an enviable business.

Despite all of the accomplishments, however, our case protagonist is not happy. Instead, he feels increasingly frustrated and withdrawn from his family and even his colleagues at work. He perceives his lack of free time as a problem; there are always demands on his time, experience, and wealth. His children think of him as a provider, but not a father. Norman, despite having what many people would envy, dreams of escaping his life.

Norman Spencer, a fictionalized character, is a composite of many successful people.

Edward M. Hallowell, a psychiatrist who practices in

Concord, Massachusetts, and teaches at Harvard Medical School, commented on Norman's story:

> "I put Norman's story together in more general terms: the very things that saved Norman—his talent and a chance to shine—are starting to destroy him. He couldn't stop shining. He couldn't regulate himself. He couldn't say no. He had no idea what to do except more of the same. He let work take over his life, not because he was greedy or selfish but because he wasn't greedy or selfish enough in the right ways. He didn't practice the basics of self-care."

The relentless pursuit of "more" in one area, will steer you away from "enough" in others. You lose your emotional connection to everything that isn't related to work.

Norman was resume-centric and thought that, by focusing intently on resume virtues, everything would fall into place, but it didn't. More work, having more things, will not solve everything; nor will they address Brooks' notion of eulogy virtues and character.

A real-life example of this single-minded focus can be found in my friend and business partner, Bob Zelinger. Bob is a partner at a large law firm in Hartford, Connecticut. When we were both younger, we focused on our careers and businesses. Bob was busy and engaged in building his successful practice. He became a sought after attorney for middle-market businesses in Connecticut. Bob was also a community leader and had the profile of a successful person. He was deeply involved in our Chamber of Commerce and went on to chair the organization with its endless meetings and events. Bob was also a board member at a large regional hospital, meaning more meetings and functions. Bob believed that being involved with these organizations, being a leader in them, would be good for his law practice, therefore he devoted many years and hours to them. Bob was successful by all measures. He guided his firm through a progression of mergers always with an improved outcome.

Like Norman Spencer, however, Bob was resume oriented. He was not spending enough time on his family and marriage—especially his marriage. Bob took his marriage for granted, ignoring the fact that marriages, like all relationships, need time, nourishment, and care. Sadly, Bob went through a painful divorce, which he considers his single biggest failure in life. When discussing this, I asked Bob if he was happy about doing all the extracurricular activities, and he pensively admitted he regretted it—too much time away from the family equaled costs that were too high, with low, if any, rewards.

Bob and I are not assailing community involvement and participation; I actually think that is part of your eulogy story. But it does need to be at the right time and in the right balance so it doesn't encroach upon top priorities.

Bob was not completely resume-centric; he had a lot of eulogy about him when it came to his children, Jeremy and Jonathan. When he was a young father, he loved making sure he was home on time to give his young children their evening bath.

Think about the juxtaposition of Bob being profiled and lauded in our local newspapers for his community leadership and professional success, and how these very activities helped undermine his marriage. Contrast that to his eulogy virtues, like the practice of giving his kids a daily bath, which was, of course, never featured in any publication.

We celebrate accomplishment and achievement—our resume virtues—but sometimes those are the very things that bring us discomfort and pain. Our eulogy virtues are largely ignored, but they are the core of our character, they drive enduring happiness and satisfaction.

MAYBE WE SHOULD GRADE CHARACTER

Ted Heavenrich, your high school advisor for three years, shared an interesting approach to amplifying focus on eulogy virtues and character. First, teach it actively in schools. Second, give kids character grades alongside academic grades.

Ted has been involved as a mentor in the Knowledge is Power Program (KIPP). A nonprofit network of college-preparatory, public charter schools serving elementary, middle, and high school students, KIPP teaches character by assigning students character grades.[26]

There has been some conversation about whether you can really grade on character traits. I'm not sure I have the answer. But teaching it, talking about it, and having some form of evaluation of it could push the focus in the right direction.

MEASURE WHAT MATTERS

Clayton Christensen is a professor at Harvard Business School. He wrote an excellent article for *Harvard Business Review* called *How Will You Measure Your Life?*[27] Based on Christensen's own personal experiences and those of his students in 2009 as the world economy faltered, it explores three questions for young students about to complete their MBA:

First, how can you be sure you will be happy in a career? Second, how can you be sure your relationships with your spouse and family become an enduring source of happiness? Third, how can you be sure you will stay out of jail (which is Christensen's way of asking how will you live a life of integrity)?

Christensen is surprised by the number of his graduate school classmates who return for reunions "unhappy, divorced, and alienated from their children." He goes on to say, "I can guarantee you that not a single one of them graduated with the deliberate strategy of getting divorced and raising children who would become estranged from them. And yet a shocking number of them implemented that strategy." Christensen attributes this to the fact that many people do not prioritize what is most important to them and misallocate their "time, talent and energy."

It's easier and more rewarding in the short term to pursue resume-like activities than eulogy-like activities, but eulogy-like activities are the ones that matter in the long run. Christensen points out that you get instant feedback, accomplishment, maybe even compensation when you invest in your career—an alluring proposition. But, building a strong marriage and raising wonderful children does not payoff for years or even decades.

Equally important, when you think about your family, it may be easy to cheat them in the short-term with little consequence, but there are ferocious long-term implications.

Christensen argues for reflecting on what matters most and allocating your time, resources, and energy to those activities and objectives.

Hopefully, you'll discover what matters most to you early enough to avoid some of the unintended outcomes Christensen's classmates experienced.

PICK THE RIGHT YARDSTICK

What makes you happy in a career? Christensen believes it's helping others and being part of something that's greater than yourself.

Jed Dorfman intentionally eschewed a more traditional career track and embraced working with kids to heal and touch their lives in a positive way. When I asked how he felt about some of his friends and peers who have built lives centered on accumulation and wealth, Jed said, "Of course I compare periodically; how can you not? But I am really happy with the choices I have made and I choose not to measure my life by money, but by character and who I am."

That's why I always tell young entrepreneurs who seek my advice that they must have something more motivating than money and doing deals. You'll achieve whatever you set your mind to do, if you're hardworking. Money, as a primary motivator, will lose its appeal once you achieve your objective. If you have a deeper purpose, however, a more meaningful motivation—like serving customers, making your community better, or making the lives of your employees better—you'll find yourself energized and engaged over the long haul.

Get the right strategy for yourself from the beginning: What do you want? Think hard about this because ultimately it will be how you measure yourself.

WRAP UP

I think you will be enormously successful at whatever you set out to do. Above all else, reflect on what yardstick you will use to measure that success and whether it's about resume or eulogy. Consider the balance of the two.

When in doubt, think about your eulogy virtues—those are the ones that reflect who you really are, not what you have accomplished.

DON'T PAY ATTENTION TO WHAT OTHERS THINK

At various times in your life, you'll be very focused on what other people think about you. This is especially true when you're younger and in highly social environments, like college. (Thankfully, as you get older, you tend to care less about what other people might think of you.) When younger, you might be concerned about how other people perceive your appearance, your clothing, what music you listen to, who your friends are, what you think, what classes you take, or any number of other things.

Here is the straight truth. You should focus on your life, your values, and doing what you think is best—even if it does not conform with what you think other people want or expect of you. Part of being a young adult is figuring out what works best for you and who you are. This is pretty hard to do, under the best of circumstances. If you layer on the constraint of trying to please other constituents, or conform to their opinion and perceptions, it becomes even more challenging.

Now, it's totally normal to want to fit in and be part of a group. When I was younger, I cared what people thought of me and often did things to meet other people's expectations. Part of this stemmed from my own insecurities and a lack of my own goals and values system. Those I interviewed, expressed the same thought: too much time and energy was spent being worried about what other people would think, especially when they were younger.

My friend, Royce Yudkoff, described this phenomenon as "needing to free yourself from what other people think." He noted that by failing to do so, you create "the equivalent of tying a dog collar around your neck and handing someone else the leash."

If you have a strong sense of self, a recognition of who you are, what you want in life, a moral compass you're comfortable with, goals, and a mission statement, you really do not need to worry about what anybody else thinks. You're on the path that's right for you, and you can ignore the noise and move forward comfortably and with confidence.

SELECT YOUR GUIDANCE RESOURCES

I'm not proposing you blindly live life without guidance or input, but carefully select and cultivate where you get your guidance and input. Preferably, you should have a handful of resources who are honest, unbiased, and truly care about you. These resources may include a mentor, sibling, parent, or very close friend. Beyond that, it's probably not worth listening to or getting down or distracted by extraneous opinions or views.

And when seeking external guidance and input, I'm not proposing you look only for confirming views. Seeking alternative perspectives is healthy and productive. But, again, strongly consider your sources of input.

For example, if you ever ask me for input or advice, I

promise you I will provide thoughts that are with your best interest at the forefront. Now, you might disagree with my ideas, and that's totally fine, but my orientation is fully genuine and objective.

NO ONE REALLY CARES

The best reason not to worry about what other people think about you: because they don't. We're all guilty of thinking we're the center of the world or more important than we really are. We're the center of our own little worlds, but beyond that, the truth is, most people really don't care about what you do or think. You might think people are talking or thinking about you, but they're not. They're focused on themselves and their own lives and worrying about what people think about them. I'm not saying this in a negative way; I'm just being realistic.

STRENGTH IN NONCONFORMITY

It's totally OK to be unconventional or conventional, as long as it works for you.

The American essayist, Ralph Waldo Emerson, believed in self-reliance, individuality, and nonconformity. Emerson argued that a person's life is his own, it doesn't belong to others; to follow your own path is life's highest calling—to follow someone else's path, puts you at risk for feeling dispirited and small. Emerson is advocating for ignoring what other people think and to follow your own heart and mind by "trusting thyself." I think Emerson's concepts argue for happiness as well as individuality.

DEFY CONVENTION

Many people who have done great and notable things have

ignored critics while having the internal resolve to drive forward based on their values, individuality, and core beliefs. I would say the ability to disregard critics, the keepers of convention, is a virtue as well.

Let me draw on an historical example of great change born on the back of defying convention. How do you think the Wright brothers felt when they were developing the seeds of modern air flight: do you think there was universal support for their initiatives? Scientific thought of the time told the Wright brothers there was no way to get done what they sought to accomplish. William Thompson (Lord Kelvin) was a leading physicist and mathematician at the University of Glasgow in the mid- to late-nineteenth century. The Scottish Hall of Fame describes him as an eminent physicist best remembered for his talent for theoretical mathematics. He's credited with formulating the second law of thermodynamics. Yet, Lord Kelvin was skeptical of flight and is attributed as saying, "I can state flatly that heavier than air flying machines are impossible." Furthermore, he declined membership in the fledgling aeronautical society claiming, "I have not the smallest molecule of faith in aerial navigation other than ballooning or of the expectation of good results from any of the trials we hear of . . . I would not care to be a member of the Aeronautical Society."

So here's a pretty smart guy who debunked the notion of flight as we know it, yet the Wright brothers ignored naysayers such as him and persisted with their project.

Orville and Wilbur Wright did not care what other people thought about their ideas or project.

When I was twenty-four years old and started my records management business, plenty of people thought it was an odd choice. Many of my friends from college and business school had professional jobs where they wore suits to work (people wore suits back then). They worked for recognized companies and had impressive titles like consultant and investment analyst. I was not in that situation at all as I labored to build my business in Waterbury, Connecticut. I felt lots of skepticism and judgment because I wasn't doing something more traditional. I was filled with doubt and uncertainty, yet I listened to my inner voice and pursued my entrepreneurial dream with vigor. It wasn't easy and I often felt like I made the wrong choice, but I persisted.

I recall at my five-year college reunion talking to a friend and sharing the story of building my own business. My friend listened, then asked if my business was a part-time thing, something to do until I got a real job! Talk about feeling judged by others. Well, I ignored some of the outside noise and trudged on with my business to great enjoyment and satisfaction. Following my own goals and compass while shutting out the naysayers was what I needed to do and the right path for me.

WHICH WAY DO I GO

It's all well and good to say you should free yourself from societal expectations, to do your own thing, but where does that leave you?

One of the most challenging things you will face as a young adult is to determine what you want your path to be. When I think about your path, I'm not focused on your vocational choices, although that's certainly part of it; I'm thinking of your life as an aggregate. An aggregate of choices. It's time to fully open your eyes to all of your choices and options and try to consciously shed or embrace the models you have witnessed.

We're all guilty of not knowing what we don't know. So, when you think about the road you will travel, be aware that there are so many paths and models of which you're just unaware.

To address this issue, be as curious as you can be. Ask as

many questions as you can ask. Always have your eyes open and observe. Resist defaulting to your preconditioning, to the models you have seen. We are all guilty of this, too. There are so many ways to live life, and there's no one right way for you, other than the one you want and choose.

You should actively deliberate your path with great effort and energy. Don't take this lightly in any way. Life is filled with gravitational pulls; if you're not specifically cognizant of what you want your life to look and feel like, you'll begin to move in a direction that might be unintended. The often-quoted discussion in Lewis Carroll's *Alice in Wonderland* accurately captures this concept . . .

"Cat: Where are you going?

Alice: Which way should I go?

Cat: That depends on where you are going.

Alice: I don't know.

Cat: Then it doesn't matter which way you go."

Where you want to go in life matters a great deal. You should use plenty of time to set your course of direction. Once you actually know where you want to go you can delve into how to get there. But, where you want to go is, by far, the most important part of the process to contemplate.

Don't have trepidation about traveling an unconventional path. You will see that at certain chronological milestones, all your peers will tend to move together in a synchronized fashion. I'm not proposing you be different just to be different, but travel your own path and resist the pressures of conformity.

When you are in your young adult years, in your twenties, you should try to always remember that this is your life. You get one shot at it and you get to do it any way you choose to do it. It's yours and all yours. You get to own it and craft it for your happiness and satisfaction. Life is a very long game; chances are good, a year or two here or there will not impact much. So, don't be in a rush—play the game at your pace, and focus on your definition of long-term happiness.

One way to discover where your happiness lies is to try everything. Don't have preconceived notions about what you want and do not want.

It seems that humans are not always great at predicting what will make them happy—which explains why people constantly move, change jobs, and divorce. Some of these changes are evolutionary, a step forward, but many are an admission of poor decision-making. The key: consider all your options; attempt to know, without a doubt, which way you should go.

WRAP UP

You'll likely not have an internationally renowned physicist assailing you or your ideas, but your peers might give you a hard time—at least, you might think they are. March to your own beat and do what's best for you. You'll find peace and happiness. You don't need to care about what other people think to be happy. Most importantly, they're probably thinking about you far less than you're thinking about them thinking about you.

HAPPINESS

Which leads us to the Holy Grail of life: happiness. That's really the goal and purpose of life. Simplistic, I know.

I'm not prescribing what happiness is for you or anybody else—that's your challenge to discover for yourself. But whatever your definition, happiness should be your goal and destination.

Here's how you'll know when you've achieved it: happiness feels like a sense of calm in your life. You're content and fulfilled with personal relationships; if you're married, your marriage is stable and rich; you're healthy; you find satisfaction in your work; and your financial situation is calm and stress-free. Of course you can be happy before marriage and work.

Happiness feels like peace.

You might be moving towards goals and objectives, but not in a frantic or hopscotching way. It's a feeling of being content, fulfilled, and satisfied. They all link; they're all indicative of being in harmony and experiencing some type of permanent and durable fulfillment.

PUT THE WORK IN NOW FOR LONG-TERM HAPPINESS

When I say happiness, I'm referring to long-term, enduring satisfaction. Short-term pleasure is something different; while not bad, it's fleeting. Like an afternoon at an amusement park filled with thrilling rides, it's fun for sure, but not that meaningful or enduring. Compare that fleeting pleasure to learning a new skill, like a second language. The latter offers enduring satisfaction. Developing such a lifelong attribute is generally hard at first, but the benefits and joy outweigh all of the short-term effort and sacrifice in the end. These are not mutually exclusive—short-term pleasure and long-term satisfaction can coexist—but think about the balance in which they exist and how you allocate your time.

Another way to contrast short-term pleasure and long-term satisfaction or happiness is to imagine a set of cool parents and a set of strict parents. The cool parents let their kids watch excessive television and mindlessly waste hours on the Internet. The kids all eat junk food and candy and soda at breakfast, which they imagine is great. School is not emphasized and there are few rules or guidelines in the house.

If you painted this picture for me when I was ten, I would have jumped at the opportunity to have these cool parents.

Contrast this with a set of strict parents who emphasize school and education, including a second language; who prioritize reading over television and the Internet. I wouldn't have been interested in their meals of vegetables and lean proteins, a little bit of sweets, but not in excess. With those uncool parents, sports, exercise, and musical instruments are encouraged. Manners and thank you notes are part of the program. What a bore.

Seeing these two pictures of parenting style, which would you have preferred at ten? Which would you wish for at thirty? Which represents short-term pleasure? And which feels like the foundation for long-term happiness and satisfaction?

U.S. Senator Corey Booker once said, "Discipline is just choosing between what you want now, and what you want most." You could substitute the word discipline with happiness.

True happiness requires perspective and a long-term orientation. You need a plan and the ability to defer short-term wants for long-term objectives. This is where your values, goals, and mission come in.

Rick Richardson says it a bit differently: everything in life is "cause and effect." You have choices, decisions, and options along the way; and each choice, decision, and option is a cause that has an effect. Often effects are very predictable when examined objectively. Effects tend to have ripples that span out.

Put the work in now, and you can all but coast. Give up some of the short-term pleasures, and you'll find increased long-term satisfaction. So, there's another virtue I would have you pursue: think long-term, not short-term.

To illustrate, the popular and wise business author, Jim Collins, talks about the concept of a flywheel. A flywheel is defined as "a heavy revolving wheel in a machine that is used to increase the machine's momentum and thereby provide greater stability or a reserve of available power during interruptions in the delivery of power to the machine."

Now, a flywheel can be challenging to get moving from a dead standstill. But with extraordinary effort, the flywheel does indeed start to move, slowly. At times the flywheel might sputter and lose momentum, but with purpose and effort the flywheel very slowly begins to build momentum and then more momentum. This might take years to occur; but, like the tortoise, if there's consistent progress, the flywheel will start to spin. As the flywheel begins to spin more and more, and faster and faster, the effort required to accelerate the motion becomes easier. Getting a huge flywheel going can be very hard, but with time and momentum it becomes nearly effortless.

Collins talks about the flywheel concept in the context of creating change in a business—change is hard in the beginning, but the more initial effort you put in to get folks moving in a new direction, the easier it becomes to keep them headed that way.

You can also apply this concept to your own personal journey to happiness. Learning and mastering Chinese, for instance, sounds like a daunting task, one that cannot be accomplished quickly or easily. But if you progressively study the language, with daily application over several years, it can be accomplished. Not only that, but it tends to get easier and more enjoyable as you go. Much like the flywheel, you've got to put in the effort to get it going and build momentum—but once you do, it tends to drive delight.

DO NOT CONFUSE HAPPINESS WITH SUCCESS

Sometimes people trade genuine and fulfilling happiness for the material trappings of success and that can be hard to unwind, or leave you with a hollow and empty feeling. People spend so much time chasing accomplishments, they forget what it is to be a balanced human being. (You see the theme?)

As you know, I'm involved in Young Presidents' Organization, or YPO. I've made some wonderful friends through this involvement. However, in this group of business leaders, I often see people who have the outward appearance of success, but upon further examination, seem to be a bit of a mess.

Let me paint a composite picture of the sort of person I'm describing: he's an extraordinarily successful guy in his fifties or sixties, with tremendous vocational accomplishments and great wealth. Like so many people in his position, in his demographic, his great success and wealth is accompanied by a divorce or two, estranged children, and dubious health.

That is a not something I would wish on anybody. This isn't happiness; this isn't success.

Don't confuse happiness with success. You can be successful and not happy, and you can be happy and not successful. Success seems to have a bit more of a professional patina to it, whereas happiness is more holistic and embraces other parts of a life beyond career.

My friend John Kenny is intensely smart. We met in the records management industry in the late nineties—I was in my late twenties, John in his late thirties at the time. When I first met John I found it difficult to talk to him, because he moved at such a quick pace. Having attended MIT and Harvard Business School, he was always quantitative and intelligent; he loved data.

John and I were both trying to make our mark in our industry, we both succeeded in different ways. John worked at Iron Mountain, the largest company in our industry and the company that wound up purchasing my business in 2007.

I learned a lot from John in business, and more as our relationship transitioned into a personal friendship after we both left the records management industry.

John and I have shared many conversations about life, kids, business, and happiness. John's journey was one filled with great success and a meteoric rise professionally, but not until he reoriented his life did he fully understand what mattered most to him and what gave him happiness.

John has been an overachiever his entire life and enjoyed the constant approval and approbation he received from teachers as a child. He thrived on it. This need for success and approval started in elementary school and lasted into his forties. When I interviewed him for this book, he told me that, as a young adult, he was singularly focused on making money and being successful. He wanted to be famous and wealthy. He wanted to be rich and successful and have people know it— "little man's disease," he called it.

John wound up becoming wealthy and famous in business circles by working tirelessly and by being a self-described workaholic. It wasn't until he left the active business chapter of his life that he came to fully understand the relationships he built in business were not key to his happiness; and he over-invested in professional relationships, compared to personal and family relationships. His priorities were wrong.

Now, he prioritizes friendships and family and is focused on relationships that truly matter in his life. He feels fortunate to be off the corporate roller coaster, as he describes it, and able to focus on happiness.

Despite this shift, John wishes he had not been as career-focused as a young adult, he wishes he had adopted a more balanced approach to life—he encouraged his two children to embrace this wisdom.

John's intensity and unbridled ambition drove his success and achievements professionally, but at some personal costs. Knowing every choice has benefits and costs, try to understand what's motivating your behaviors, why, and what the implications of your motivations and actions are.

Rick Ruback, a professor, has dedicated his career to training and developing promising young adults so they can have productive lives. Two of his children became teachers as well. His daughter, Rose, is a public high school teacher and derives great fulfillment and satisfaction from this path. His son, Ben, who also teaches high school, has faced some health challenges. Ben enjoyed teaching so much that he arranged his healthcare activities in a way to ensure he was in class as much as possible. Rick's kids do not choose to measure the quality of their lives by money. They're focused on a different form and level of happiness and satisfaction. Rick pointed out that his children might not have the same income levels as some of his MBA students, but they're OK with that. They enjoy the lives they've constructed. Less income is a cost they're willing to pay for career satisfaction and personal happiness.

HABITS OF HAPPY PEOPLE

I encourage you to intentionally and deliberately search for and embrace activities that fill you with happiness and satisfaction, even if they offer you some challenge, even if it takes you a good deal of time to discover them. This intentionality will help you best think about and figure out how to use your precious time.

There's another virtue: be intentional.

At times, we invest more time and thought into what Netflix movie to watch than some really important and impactful decisions in life. Maybe that's why many I spoke with used the word deliberate, or some variation of that word, when discussing choices and happiness.

Charlie Saponaro has a handful of ways he behaves deliberately to bring joy into his life. One consists of a detailed spreadsheet, which highlights things in his life that give him fulfillment and happiness. He purposefully details an activity and how to make it happen. Charlie also keeps a daily journal in which he records what he's grateful for and what he did to make the day great. He has a morning routine that includes some physical movement, meditation, and envisioning what the day will be like and what he's grateful for. The man is deliberate.

Happy people are better masters of their time. They know they have only so many hours in a day, so much bandwidth, so they choose their activities carefully. There are some great tools to help you do this—here are two examples:

- **The Three-Pronged Model**. Matt Guyer uses a simple three-pronged model to assess whether something is a good allocation of time and likely to bring happiness: Do I like it? Is it good for me? Is it costly?

Let's look at three test cases . . .

Hiking. I really enjoy it; it's good for me, because I'm outside, in nature, being active; and it's free—wow! That one is an easy win.

Devouring a giant hot fudge sundae. I sure do like it; it's not so good for me; and it's relatively cheap. Might be OK as a periodic indulgence, but not something that should be a regular habit.

An exotic vacation. I sure would enjoy it; it would probably be good for me because it would expand my understanding of cultures; but likely it would be expensive. Seems like something to aspire to do infrequently, as a special opportunity.

Drinking too much alcohol. I do not enjoy it; it's certainly not good for me; and it can be cheap or expensive. I'll pass—it appears to miss too many tests.

I'm not prescribing what's right or wrong here, just offering you a quick way to determine whether you're deliberatively engaging in activities that move you along to happiness and satisfaction, or not.

I might expand Matt's useful model to include a fourth dimension: who are you sharing the time and activity with? If the people you're interacting with lift you up and bring you joy, that's another great reason to jump in. If the people are energy consumers or bring you down, best to avoid the activity.

- **The Four-Quadrant Model.** Stephen Covey, author of the popular 7 *Habits of Highly Effective People*, uses a four-quadrant model[28] to think about how people should use their time. The screens (or filters) he uses to place an activity in each quadrant are "what is urgent?" and "what is important?" Here's a look at my interpretation of these quadrants:

	Urgent	**Not Urgent**
Important	*Quadrant 1: Manage time here* • Reacting to fire drills and crises • Meeting deadlines without long preparation • Reacting mode	*Quadrant 2: Focus time here* • Thoughtful planning • Relationships that matter • Thinking about and reflecting on values • Focusing on health and spirituality
Not Important	*Quadrant 3: Limit time here* • Unimportant meetings • False crises • Unnecessary disruptions • Reacting to someone else's urgencies	*Quadrant 4: Avoid time here* • Wasting time • Busy work • Surfing the Internet aimlessly • Excessive TV or other indulgences

Thinking about who you are and where you want to go in life is a Covey quadrant two activity—it's really important, and will have great implications, but it's not an urgent matter. It can always be deferred for a day or even a year. But this is exactly where you should be spending a good portion of your time. Otherwise, you risk being Alice-like and it not mattering which way you head.

Ken Saxon, who chuckles as he says he's been working on self-development for over thirty years, thinks *The 7 Habits of Highly Effective People* was the single most important book he read in his twenties; and he's currently reading the book, again, along with his two children who are finishing college.

WRAP UP

Pay close attention to how you define happiness and fulfillment and how you will find it—this is one of the single most important questions you will answer as a young adult. Happiness and success are two very different notions and it's important you remember that although these concepts are often comingled, and used interchangeably, they are independent. Be deliberate in your choices and how you allocate your time. As a young adult, you might fear missing out on something. You'll want to be at every event, party, and social gathering. Just make sure you engage in the activities that make sense for you; that you spend your precious time with the people you want to be with. There are only so many hours in a day; you must choose how to use them well.

EMBRACE THE PROCESS

If I could suggest to you one thing that will most affect your happiness in life, it might be this: adopt the long game mentality. You've seen me speak to it before, but let me expound upon it here.

Sometimes in life you can get very focused on goals and outcomes. This is why it's so easy to focus on accomplishments rather than character; why resume virtues get all the press, and eulogy virtues are all but ignored. This is why it's so easy to think short-term; you're simply moving from goal post to goal post, without thinking about the big picture.

While pursuing goals is important and positive, being that they're one of those building blocks to your happiness and success, you also need to embrace and relish the journey.

Sometimes you experience a huge let down when you achieve a goal. This can happen for several reasons. One, what you thought you would feel upon triumph is not exactly what you feel. Two, you enjoyed the process of working towards the goal a lot more than the attainment of the goal. Third, whatever you thought the goal would bring you is less fulfilling and satisfying than you imagined.

I often talk to entrepreneurs about goal achievement. I try to explain that when you build a business, the best mindset to have is one of an architect—you really enjoy building and cannot wait to get up every day to design and develop.

Contrast this to someone who thinks about business exclusively as a means to accumulate money. In this case, money is a goal and an outcome. The process isn't emphasized as much, or at all. Only the goal matters.

Well, at some point, if you're a good entrepreneur you'll realize you have hit your goal of accumulating a certain amount of money. If that was all that was driving or motivating you, you'll quickly feel empty; you won't want to pop out of bed. If you're an architect and a builder, money might be used as a measure of the health of the business, but it is not the sole driver of why you wake up. Rather, it's the process and journey that excite and motivate you.

Ray Allen, who won two NBA titles, said the thrill of winning a title is very fleeting. If you're only chasing that high, you'll be very depressed. Championships are secondary to the feeling you get from putting in the work every day and embracing the process. Allen states that true happiness in the championship is the winding path you take—the process.[29]

When I sold my first business, it was a bit anticlimactic. The sale itself was validating, but I'm not sure that was ever really my goal. I loved the process of building and creating, of being the architect. That's where my professional happiness was, not the outcome itself.

Whatever your goals, I hope they're meaningful in your life, and you enjoy the process along the way. That's where true joy is found.

LIFE IS A MARATHON, NOT A SPRINT

You're about to embark on the long marathon of life, and it's an amazing journey. Compared to a sprint, a marathon is a long trek, there's no rush. You have plenty of time. Don't squander time, mind you, but there's no need to be hasty either.

When Mike Erwin was a young adult, he had a "restless sense of urgency and a need to get stuff done." He now wishes he had taken a longer view of life and had not been in such a rush to shape his own success. That burning sense of urgency just was not necessary and he did not need to live "like his hair was on fire."

Jed Dorfman, who runs a youth summer camp in New Hampshire, noted that many of the Australian and New Zealander counselors at his camp take one to five years post college to travel and see the world before actually beginning their "real" life. Unlike their American counterparts, they resist the notion that they're falling behind, because they're not. What these global travelers are doing is building experiences and memories that will last a lifetime, experiences and memories that will shape them, and be cherished when they're ninety. I think we would all do well to slow down and experience the world before sprinting into life.

When I was in my mid-twenties, I wanted to get going in a big way. I, too, was in a needless rush. I wanted too much, too quickly, and it probably catalyzed some mistakes and missed opportunities.

We have a bias towards action and doing in our culture. Yet sometimes the best decision is to not do something, at least temporarily. If you react from pure emotion, with too much excitement or fear, you may put yourself in a compromised position. Pause, and you will likely make fewer mistakes. As Peter Kies says, "Stay the course and avoid being impatient. Nothing good comes from hasty, impatient actions and decisions."

THE TORTOISE AND THE HARE THING AGAIN

So much of happiness and life is about steady and consistent progress, avoiding fits and starts. There's another virtue: be the tortoise, steady and consistent.

Think of the many skills you have acquired to date: Spanish fluency, deliberately acquired over six years with annual progression; nothing dramatic or splashy, just a consistent application. Playing the piano, same routine.

It's generally not possible to move forward in hare-like fashion and expect desirable results. Meaningful friendships take years to develop, nurture, and bind. Most skills take years of diligent adherence to master. Financial accumulation is about decades of saving and wise investing. Starting and stopping in fits like the hare is a sure way to lose momentum and energy.

When you become proficient at something, it is done with ease and confidence, but obtaining proficiency is arduous and time consuming. If you behave like the hare, starting and stopping activities, or bouncing from one venue to another, you'll never fully give yourself the opportunity to let the seeds you have planted fully ripen and mature. Everybody thinks there are hare-like ways to get ahead in life; rarely are there. The tortoise represents unglamorous triumph in fables and in life. But I'll take triumph, unglamorous or otherwise, every time.

Several years ago we had the unique opportunity to meet with John Bogle, the founder of Vanguard—the investment behemoth. Bogle changed the way many people think about investments and revolutionized the investment industry. He shifted the generally accepted strategy from active investment management to passive investment management. In our conversation with Bogle, he must have used the phrase "stay the course" at least a dozen times. Obviously, he was using this in the context of an investment philosophy, but I think his view of "stay the course" can be embraced in many parts of your life. The tortoise stayed the course; the hare did not. I interpret Bogle's philosophy of staying the course to be defining your objectives, deciding how you are going to implement action steps to achieve your objectives, and then sticking to your program unwaveringly. A lot of life is just staying the course.

LOOKING AHEAD

Envisioning what your life will look like can be challenging, even overwhelming, but it's the single most important thing you can use your time for in your twenties. Think of it as the best kind of life insurance.

It will be very hard for you to use this screen, but attempt to do things in your young life that will drive and augment your happiness when you're in your fifties, sixties, and beyond. (I touched on this looking ahead thing in the careers chapter.) It must be painful and depressing to be in your seventies and not have had a happy life; to have to look back on regrets, should haves, and could haves. Your definition of happiness might evolve over time, and that's OK, but focus on happiness.

Try to think a few innings ahead and understand how you will be happy in the future. Royce Yudkoff suggests directing yourself on a course for your needs when you're older, and to eschew the easiest path when you're younger. The key is to figure out where you want to be and what you want your life to look like and then organize your activities and energies as best as possible to propel yourself in that direction.

Think about moments when you feel happiest, Royce suggests, and attempt to tease out exactly what is driving that emotion. *Is it explicitly what you're doing, or is being part of a team working together with a common cause? Is it the people you're with and the associated intellectual stimulation, or something else?* This will inform your happiness now, and later.

PIVOT POINTS

It's healthy to slow down, pause, and do a large amount of introspection to really get at what you want.

John Hayes, CEO of Ball Corporation, a Fortune 500 company based in Colorado, recently gave a talk at the University of Denver. In sharing his story and journey towards happiness, John talked about "pivot points"—those moments in life when you pause and decide whether to make a left turn or a right turn or to keep going straight.[30]

While at Lehman Brothers, his first job out of business school, he experienced a horrible jet-skiing accident. Facial reconstructive surgery and a two-month hospital stay gave him a lot of time on his hands. He began to assess where he was in life. Although a very successful investment banker, John wasn't happy. What he had envisioned as his dream job was not, in fact, fun. He traveled too much, and rarely had time to spend with his newborn child, Annie. He also didn't like the transactional nature of his work.

John's unintentional two-month sabbatical catalyzed a pivot point in his life. He suddenly had the time and space to contemplate where he fit in the world, what motivated him, what he valued, and how to find a higher purpose.

Shortly after he recovered, John left Lehman Brothers and joined Ball, a job that gave him personal and professional fulfillment. Ball was an organization in which John felt he could balance his personal and professional goals. There, he was able to engage in a people-centric orientation as opposed to a transaction-centric one. At Ball, John was part of a team, an important member of a far more purposeful workplace. This made him incredibly happy.

John found great satisfaction and success after that pivot point, but the most important part of the anecdote is that John paused and reflected on what he wanted in life. Despite his success at Lehman, he knew the position wasn't right for him. Only with intentional deliberation did John find the right course. Without reflection, John would have charged ahead, doing what he was doing, pulled by one of life's many gravitational forces.

At times, life will deal you good cards, other times, bad cards. What you do next is the real reflection of who you are and how you make the most of the situation in which you find yourself.

WRAP UP

I strongly encourage you to think about happiness purposefully and in a conscious manner. When you think about finding happiness in life, think about how the tortoise won the race; how the hare lost it, as well as their different styles and approaches. Think about the flywheels in your life and how good you will feel when they're spinning easily, but also what it takes to get your flywheels building momentum and energy. Finding enduring satisfaction and happiness is not always easy, it does take effort. But if you're pursuing your dreams and goals, the effort is worth it. It gets easier and is rewarded.

FAILURE

Failure is going to be part of your life, so you might as well get used to it and embrace it. To think you'll coast through life without experiencing failure is optimistic, but also naïve. All people pursuing happiness or greatness trip, regularly, and experience failure. Unless you have very low aspirations and expectations in your life, you'll experience failure and lots of it. Your failures will happen in personal relationships, academic settings, athletic endeavors, and professional situations. Failure will take place in all aspects of your life, regularly.

You have already gotten a taste for this. As a freshman in high school, it was a great achievement that you made the junior varsity soccer team; people were impressed and congratulated you. You played on that team for the next two years, biding your time in anticipation of making the jump to varsity. As a junior, you hoped to make the leap, but it didn't happen. This was disappointing for you, but you handled the situation with maturity and balance. You played your junior year with enthusiasm and spirit and embraced the situation for all of its opportunity. Finally, as a senior you made the varsity soccer team, which is fantastic, but it was probably a slower progression than you would have liked.

At the end of your freshman year, you auditioned for a select choral group at school. I was so impressed and proud of you for moving outside your comfort zone. I thought it was fantastic, you trying out for something you'd never tried before. Truthfully, I was excited, and surprised, when you were selected for the group. When your sophomore year started, the singing group began rehearsals, and you jumped right in. After a few practice sessions, the instructor asked you to leave the group. Wow, that was rough. Mom and I felt so bad for you and were a bit shocked that, after being selected, you were being dropped! That was an unpleasant situation for you, but failure is just part of what happens in life. You reacted with some chagrin and dismay initially, and then just moved on without giving it another thought.

This ability to shrug it off will serve you well. Failure can catalyze opportunity, too. When you left the singing group you joined a service learning class and had meaningful experiences working at a Waterbury elementary school, which might not have happened otherwise.

OUR RISK-AVERSE CULTURE

I'm not espousing that failure is easy, fun, or should be sought out, but you do need to be prepared for it. Part of the reason we're all so failure-averse is that we're trained in school, from a very young age, to move in a linear path, one that makes no room for deviation—for failing. We move along this smooth and pre-established path where the basic message is "do what you are told and you will progress." Failure is viewed as something very bad, something not to be tolerated (let alone celebrated or part of experimentation or exploration).

There are exceptions, of course.

A few years ago I had the privilege of visiting the U.S. Military Academy at West Point, where Jim Collins presented to the entire student body. It was a fantastic session, but one thing stood out in my mind particularly: Collins asked the students, "Have you learned or experienced failure at West Point?"

Every single person in the room raised his or her hand; there were a lot of smiles and chuckles, as well.

This is a group of elite young adults who will be our future military leaders and strategists and they all recognize that failure is part of learning and growing; it's part of their education.

The 'don't-fail' mindset continues when you get out of school; you cannot escape it, even when you think you're taking the path least traveled.

FAILURE IS NOT ABOUT BEING DUMB

When you fail, and you will, you should keep in mind that life is never a smooth and straight path, and failure is often not "your fault."

I've seen smart people with great success make big mistakes. It doesn't mean they're suddenly dumb or careless; it just means that something didn't work out as they had planned.

I've been in many situations where I used the same successful tools and techniques that worked well in the past, only to discover in a new context, they just don't work.

Consider former President Bill Clinton. In 1974, he ran for Congress and lost—a failure. In 1976, he was elected Attorney General in Arkansas—a success. In 1978, he was elected Governor of Arkansas—a success. In 1980, he lost in his re-election bid for Governor of Arkansas—a failure. In 1982, he was re-elected as Governor of Arkansas and went on to become a two-term U.S. president—the ultimate success, one might think.

Early failures did not deter Clinton. He regrouped and moved forward. Failures are just part of everybody's arc and path. The only thing dumb about them is if they cause you to give up.

FAILURE AS COURSE CORRECTION

Sometimes we need a failure to help us reorient and get back on track. Your uncle, Reuben Daniels, for example, was once fired from a prestigious investment-banking job at Barclays. Although Reuben was clearly upset about what had happened, he realized he was the same person he was when he quickly rose in his career—accumulating responsibility, promotions, compensation, and positive feedback—as the man who was fired.

Keep this in mind when you experience failure. Even when you encounter failure, you're still the same person who experienced wins. Most importantly, if you do experience a failure or setback, the time may be right to analyze and think about what happened: why did the failure take place?

It's also appropriate to reflect and prioritize.

When Reuben was pushed out of Barclays, he had an abrupt change in his life, and it was a very painful one. As was the case with John Hayes and his forced sabbatical after his jet-skiing accident, Reuben had to pause. This pause, however, gave him the opportunity to see what he really wanted in life. Reuben looked at his family life and his relationships with his children, your cousins, and made the decision to restructure. Instead of attempting to replicate his previous iteration—a globetrotting, deal-making, always-on-the-go banker—he started his own business, drawing upon his experiences and background.

No longer part of a global organization, his world changed, but for the better. He focused on family. He became a better father and husband. Not only did he become more engaged in his children's lives, he did so in a more meaningful way with improved communication and listening skills, a gift of having worked on these issues.

If you do not see something—an activity, a relationship, a job, an environment—helping propel you towards happiness and success, stop and examine the problem carefully. Consider the possibility that you may have made a mistake. Pause, consider, and course correct.

So often failures can initially seem debilitating, but frequently with time a failure is just one step thrusting us forward, often in a better way. Of course, you do not need to wait for a failure in order to evaluate and consider.

WHEN YOU JUST SCREW UP

Sometimes failures are self-inflicted, and the result of losing track of your way.

A few years ago, I got involved at Onesource Water. As I was orienting myself at the company, a meeting was scheduled in Orlando, Florida, on November twelfth—your sister Leah's birthday. I made the choice to attend the meeting anyway, despite the disappointment it would cause her.

Going to that meeting in Orlando, missing my daughter's seventh birthday, was a failure. Mom chastised me for attending the meeting and I brushed it off. I felt I needed to be at the meeting in light of my new CEO role. Mom, of course, was correct (as usual); I was completely in the wrong. I failed as a father, my most important role. I deeply regret that decision. I know my failure stemmed from having lost my priorities and compass.

So, failures can come in multiple forms. Self-inflicted failures, however, are the worst, because they're typically avoidable.

IT MAY NOT BE YOU

When you think about success and failure, remember that it's not all about you. To be successful in any endeavor, personal or professional, there's a large cast and network that supports you. Teachers, coaches, teammates, peers, friends, colleagues, parents, bosses, mentors, and good luck all play a role in your successes and wins. It's naïve and foolish for anybody to think their accomplishments are exclusively self-made and fully independent. You might have the starring role in a win, but there's a large group of people helping boost you upward.

Of course, you should always thank, appreciate, and acknowledge that support system.

Analogously, when you fail, you're the very same person and likely had a support system and network helping you, but for some reason, it didn't work.

You don't win alone, and you don't fail alone. What matters is you're still the same person, and hopefully a good one.

ROUGH TRANSITIONS

Sometimes, what looks and feels like a failure is nothing more than the growing pains of transition. Transitions are hard and college is one of those big resets in life where what you did in your last chapter doesn't matter that much anymore.

In high school, Jed Dorfman was a hero and a rock star. Captain of this team, president of that organization, top of his academics—he had all bases covered. He was the whole package. When he arrived at college, however, his star lost its shine and he began to struggle academically, athletically, and socially. He felt lost, like he had failed. He described himself as the classic hero to zero in the high school to college jump.

Jed left college after his freshman year and spent some time in Colorado thinking about where he was and how to reorient. After an out of sequence gap year, Jed returned to college in a better place and subsequently had a more positive experience. Notice how this pause-and-reevaluate concept keeps cropping up.

Failures happen all the time, to everybody; they're not insurmountable. And sometimes transitions seem like failures, when really you just need to pause, readjust, and plan how to move forward.

A HEALTHY FEAR OF FAILURE

Yes, we operate in a failure-averse society, and there's a real downside to that. But there's also an upside to it, as well: fear can be a powerful motivator.

Here's what Marjorie Dorr has to say about it:

> "I do fear failure, but that is what makes me in fact 'lean in' and succeed when things get tough or I begin to fear failure. It makes me work harder; I reach out to people and ask for help (she would rather appear less smart than to fail); I start working contingency plans; I look at other options; and then, inevitably, things begin to work out, maybe differently than I originally envisioned, but it's usually a better outcome that is shared with others that I have engaged. So, a healthy fear of failure is good. It has helped me achieve more than I thought possible because I don't quit too soon. It has also helped me build a wide community of support—people love to help, they feel flattered—and it's opened up more possibilities for alternative solutions.

> "But, failure also has consequences, and it's important that young adults understand, learn, and feel the consequences, not in a way that keeps them from trying new things, but in a way that keeps them from making reckless choices."

Being afraid of failure to the point of inaction is bad, but a healthy dose of fear may be just the thing needed to motivate you towards success.

THE ABILITY TO HANDLE ADVERSITY

How you behave when you face adversity, the very real possibility of failure, says a lot about your character. Marjorie Dorr rose in her organization because she doubles down when she meets an obstacle; she gets smart.

Recently, I read an article in *The New York Times* about the Chicago Cubs and their great success during the 2016 baseball season.[31] The article explored Theo Epstein, the Cubs President of Baseball Operations, and his approach to selecting players for the team. Epstein is well known for delivering two World Series championships in Boston, one in 2004, the other in 2007, through his quantitative approach to player selection.

When screening whom to add to the team, Epstein not only focuses on raw data reflecting a player's physical abilities, but also the player's personal characteristics. Specifically, he's most focused on assessing how potential players confront adversity. Epstein and the Cubs staff require three examples of how a potential player addressed adversity on the field, how he responded; and they require three examples of how that potential player addressed adversity off the field. If they can't demonstrate an ability to handle failure—on and off the field—they're not selected for the team.

Major League Baseball is just one example. There's no question, adversity and failure exist even at the highest levels of success. As Theo Epstein knows, the question is how you react in the face of that adversity and failure.

FAILING UP

Failure is just part of success. Think of all the baseball players who strike out far more than they hit. If you look at a list of all-time strikeout heroes (led by Reggie Jackson, by the way) it looks like a Who's Who of Hall of Famers.

Thomas Edison is reputed to have failed 1,000 times during his attempt to develop the light bulb. When asked about how he felt about that, he's said to have replied, "I didn't fail 1,000 times. The light bulb was an invention with 1,000 steps."

Basketball star, Ray Allen, recently wrote a letter to himself—from his forty-one-year-old-self, to his younger, thirteen-year-old self.[32]   One of the points he makes in the letter is that he took 26,000 shots in his basketball career, 60 percent of which missed and did not go in the hoop.

Ray, sounding very much like Edison, reflects that success is cloaked in failure; success is built on a thousand failures.

THE FULCRUM OF RISK AND FAILURE

One way to think about failure is in the context of risk. If you take on a lot of risk, the probability of failure may be higher. If you take on no risk, you're likely to avoid failure. Finding that fulcrum of risk and failure is tricky. You should not unconditionally avoid risk, just imprudent risk.

When you think about risk and failure, Royce Yudkoff advises you to "take prudent and thoughtful risks and do not waste time thinking about problems two to three steps ahead that are not immediately actionable." But please be prepared for setback and failure, because they're inevitable, a question of when, not if.

When Ted Heavenrich was a young adult, he was too timid around risk and didn't fail enough, or take enough chances in his life. In retrospect, he wishes he would have taken more risks.

If you have some amount of ambition in your life, there's a chance you'll fail at times. I think you need to accept that setbacks and failures will happen, and determine if the potential for failure is acceptable or not at certain points of your life.

To Brad Hutensky, the important part of failure is learning from the experience and deciding, in advance, how you're going to react if you do fail. Will you pause, reflect, and move forward; or will you shrink, go to a dark place, and hide? That's the question.

LIFE MOVES ON

One of the benefits of being older is that you can look back and see that nothing is ever as awful as it seems. All those things you thought were complete disasters and you would never recover from, you in fact did. No matter the setback or failure, life does move on. Whether it's a broken romantic relationship, a missed professional opportunity, or an academic class that went the wrong way, it's not the end.

Jason Pananos wishes that when he was in his early twenties, he wasn't as fearful of rejection and failure. He advises that you don't let rejection impact you—there's just too much of it. Whether it's asking a girl out on a date and experiencing the painful sting of hearing no, or not getting that dream job, keep moving on, and never let the rejection or failure dissuade you or falsely convince you that it's a permanent setback.

So don't worry. Even when you find yourself in the darkest of times, remember: it's going to be OK; even dark times ultimately resolve themselves.

IT GETS EASIER TO LAUGH AT YOURSELF

Let's face it: sometimes failure is funny.

In the words of Steve Levitt, of *Freakonomics* fame:

> "I think to be willing to accept failure, you have to have self-confidence. You have to be accepting of the idea that failing doesn't define who you are. Failing gets something out of the way, that keeps

you from finding the thing that you're actually going to be good at. I mean, look, we're spoiled, you and I both have both stumbled onto a lot of success and it's so much easier to be terrible at things and to admit you are terrible when in other parts of your life you get rewarded and people write you letters and say you're great. I think it's easy for us to accept failure. And honestly, I think I've gotten much better as I've gotten older at being able to laugh at myself. I was really insecure for a long time. I didn't want to show people I was bad. But now I think I've actually gotten . . . I mean, I often will laugh the hardest when I do stupid things."

The good news: it gets easier to laugh at yourself (and your failures) the older you get.

WRAP UP

Failure will be a part of everything you do. Don't get dejected by it—get used to it. Sometimes you'll have to make the best of whatever situation you're in.

If you're not experiencing failure and rejection, you're not trying hard enough or reaching high enough. Rejection and failure are normal. You need to learn from it—remembering it will all work out in the end, either fortuitously or through effort. Your job is to just keep moving forward.

WHEN YOU SHOULD GIVE UP

As you may recall, grit is a laudable character trait—but you should also know when to quit and give up.

There will be times in your life when you're engaged in a project or a relationship and you encounter a moment that—despite all of your positive energy, persistence, and intellect—you recognize something just isn't working, and you don't see how it will ever work. That's a good moment to switch gears and figure out how you can gracefully end the situation or extract yourself.

I'm not suggesting you easily give up or not be tenacious, but there are times when things will not work and you should stop expending effort to try to make them work. It will no longer be a productive use of your time, energy, or resources. Holding on too long in these circumstances can be a mental and an emotional drain, even a financial black hole.

Your bias should always be to persist, but know when to stop, too.

To give up, or not give up, that is the question.

ASK YOURSELF THESE QUESTIONS

A good way to test whether it might be time to move on in a situation is to ask the following questions:

- Have I done everything I could to make this situation a success?

- What resources, or assistance, could I bring to the situation that I haven't already tried?

- Have facts or information about the situation changed in some way?

- Can I envision a positive outcome in some way?

If you feel you have done everything you possibly can to make the situation a success, and it still doesn't look like you can get to success, it might be time to stop.

If you cannot bring more resources—time, money, focus, energy, outside help—to a situation to improve it, it might be time to stop.

If the facts, circumstances, or information about the situation have changed significantly enough that you would not engage in the situation knowing what you know now, it might be time to stop.

Finally, if there's not a way you can envision a positive outcome, no matter what you do, it might be time to stop.

When you commit to a decision or course of action it's human nature to feel invested and even compelled to stay beyond what makes sense. The Spanish word for worthwhile, *vale la pena*, literally translates into English as *worth the pain*.

There are many things in life that are worth the pain: studying to learn and do well in school, exercising to be healthy and enjoy physical activity, nurturing a relationship to enjoy the personal connection. These are just a few examples. Sometimes things aren't worth the pain. You'll have to think about this. When it's not worth the pain, you should figure out how to stop the pain.

Sometimes when you stop a situation, or quit, you'll let people down, including yourself. You'll likely feel remorse or a sense of failure. I'm not sure there is a way to combat those feelings. Yet, despite those emotions, sometimes stopping is the right thing to do.

SOME THINGS ARE "CHEAP" TO CHANGE

As discussed previously, where you live is a big decision in your life—it's also a terrific example of something you may consider changing, with relatively few consequences, at one or more points in your life.

If you find yourself in a situation where you've thought rationally and diligently about where to live, you've invested time and energy into your new community, worked to build friendships, but after several years, you're unhappy, you should give up and change.

Sometimes it takes the most courage to admit you were wrong. In this case, being in a place you don't find fulfilling for the life you want is an easily correctable situation: just move.

By all means change, but try to learn what about your initial decision went wrong and how you can prevent repeating the same faulty analysis and decision-making. The costs of being wrong and the precipitated change, at least in this case, aren't impossible.

SOME THINGS ARE VERY "EXPENSIVE" TO CHANGE

Marriage is probably the most difficult thing to give up on. I'm very lucky to be in a caring, loving, and happy marriage, but many people are not. The divorce rate in the United States is about 50 percent. Some just quit trying; but others have done everything possible and they know—despite all they'll lose—they'll ultimately gain more by giving up on the union. This is especially true if the people in the marriage are confronting drug or alcohol addiction, gambling, abusive physical or psychological dynamics, or severe mental illness.

First of all, don't take ending a marriage lightly. Dissolving a marriage appears to be painful and emotionally charged. If children are involved, it's often very destructive for them.

Obviously, I wouldn't wish a bad marriage on anyone, especially you. But if you find yourself in a negative marriage situation; if you do everything possible to make that marriage work (including seeking professional help); and if, after everything you do, there is no progress, no indication of a positive outcome, it might make sense to end the relationship and move on.

The salient point here is that even when something as important as a marriage needs to be abandoned, life will be OK—as long as you believe you've put everything you can into the situation to make it positive. Don't be afraid to quit when you think it's the best choice. Hanging on too long can be painful and unnecessary.

MY OWN DESECISION TO LET GO

Let me share a trying situation I was in, one in which I ultimately made the decision to let go. It was a difficult decision, and not something I'm particularly proud of. But in retrospect, it was absolutely the correct choice, one I probably should have made much earlier . . .

In September 2013, I became the CEO of Onesource Water, a company where I was an investor and a board member. The company, facing some very difficult challenges, needed new leadership. The board asked if I would step into that role. After demurring, I succumbed to my ego and vanity and agreed.

Turns out, the company was in far worse shape than

anybody understood, including me. The company was losing about $4 million per year; and there was no harmony amongst the board members, investors, and executive management team on the right strategy and direction for the company. It was a complete circus. I do not assign blame to other people—at least part of the chaos had to be my fault; I was the CEO.

Over a three-year period, I made drastic changes in the company, including letting people go who weren't aligned with the values, refinancing the balance sheet, and achieving annual profitability of about $9.2 million.

The company was in a better place and I persevered through sheer grit, but there was still disharmony amongst board members and investors about what to do with the business. I felt like it was absolutely impossible to make all of my constituents happy—no matter what I did—and the situation was adversely impacting my health.

Ultimately, we decided to sell the business, which I believed was the right strategy. The board waffled several times and at one point decided not to sell. I did a lot of soul searching and told the board that if we didn't sell the business, I needed to resign. I didn't want to be in an environment that was so chaotic and dysfunctional, despite the improvements in the base business.

So, I quit.

It was a very painful decision with some good consequences (the board reconsidered and did sell the business), and some bad consequences (my resignation caused a renegotiation with our banks that proved to be very expensive and I strained some personal relationships with people involved in the business).

I felt I did everything I could to reposition the business to a better place, to try and build consensus around our strategy, but I couldn't. I don't consider myself a quitter, but in this situation, it was unequivocally the right thing to do—I only wish I'd done it earlier. I'm much happier and have extricated myself from a very stressful situation. As always, life goes on.

WRAP UP

If a situation you're in is toxic and you feel that no matter how much effort you put in, it cannot be remedied, think hard about exiting the situation.

Of course, when you do need to resign or unwind a situation, do it in a way that's caring, thoughtful, and fair. Don't leave another person in a bind; don't exit in a way that would be considered malicious or harmful. Life is a long journey and even when something isn't working, you can and should wrap it up in as harmonious and pleasant a way as possible.

I encourage you to exhibit grit and bring all of your energy and intellect to make everything in which you're involved positive and successful, but there will be times when the very best thing for you to do is give up and quit. Don't take that decision lightly; but don't eliminate it as a potential choice. Learn from what went wrong, of course, but quitting is an acceptable choice—sometimes it's the very best, smartest, and healthiest choice.

SOMETHING BIGGER
THAN YOU

Many people interviewed for this project attribute part of their happiness to having a spiritual or religious component in their life. They claim this element makes them better able to discover and embrace who they are, separate the white noise from what matters most to them. Perhaps having a religious or spiritual practice might help you, as well—to clear your thoughts and experience deep, lasting happiness and success. To better know yourself.

Sometimes in life you can feel lonely, even if people surround you. From time to time, life can be filled with failure, doubt, and disappointment; no one gets a free pass. Many people find strength and solace, particularly during rocky times, in the notion there's something bigger than themselves. Religion and spirituality can offer you paths to a sense of connection and belonging; and a way to further explore your values, character, and positive mindset.

Our rabbi, Eric Polokoff, would say that when you embrace something bigger than yourself, when you don't focus exclusively on you as an individual, you're more open to understanding how you fit into a bigger picture and context. Marjorie Dorr calls it being part of a larger ecosystem that's truly bigger than our individual self.

Let's discuss religion and spirituality. I often think of religion and spirituality as being different, with linked concepts. You can be religious without being spiritual, and you can be spiritual without being religious. I personally am pretty curious about the spiritual components of religion and think that, in the bustle of life, attention to it gets lost. You'll find what mix and balance works best for you as your life unfolds. Of course, like most things, the balance will morph.

Mom and I are not particularly religious, but I hope we're spiritual and reflective. In some ways, I'm not fully sure we've figured out where religion fits into our lives. Denise deFiebre is much clearer on the topic. She feels religion is a channel where you can get in touch with your intrinsic self. Her religious practices are an opportunity to hear herself and reorder her life, while making sure the most important things in her life are at the top of the list.

Danny Rosen finds comfort in knowing he's a link in a religious chain that goes back thousands of years. Danny believes religion has provided him with a compass for how to live and interact with people. It's helped establish values for him and his family. Religion, for Danny, helps differentiate right from wrong.

I think the purpose of most religions is to provide a framework to live a good life and to establish certain mores for positive and negative behavior. As an example, the Ten Commandments instruct you what to do (and what not to do), with the purpose of making your life easier to live.

If I had to distill religion down to a simple sentence, it would be the Golden Rule: do unto others as you would to yourself. Or more simply, treat people the way you would like to be treated.

Interestingly, this maxim appears in many religions across geography and time. I guess this implies that philosophers and religious leaders often came to a similar conclusion, that this principle is a guiding precept for religious and spiritual behavior.

When you think about religion—and life in general—this is a pretty compelling light. If you can generally think about treating people how you would like to be treated, you're likely to be doing the right thing. It'll be interesting to see how you orient religion and spirituality in your life.

THREE BUCKETS OF RELIGION

I think the broad topic of religion can be split up into three more defined buckets: ceremonial religious components, cultural components, and spiritual components.

Ceremonial religious components are the rituals and formal rhythms that define a religion: going to church daily or weekly; reciting specific prayers in a specific order; celebrating Rosh Hashanah, the Jewish New Year, in a temple.

Cultural components of religions exist within entire religious groups and within certain sub-ethnic religious groups. These are often the non-religious components of a religious celebration: what you eat on a certain holiday; what you wear when attending church; the stories you share around a certain holiday or religious event.

Spiritual Components of religion are more personal and amorphous. This is the part of religion where the individual contemplates his or her role in a broader world: who and what God is, and the individual's relationship to God.

The spiritual dimension of religion can also explore how a person fits into nature and finds peace and calm. This sense of oneness can be found in a contemplative hike in the woods, kayaking on a calm lake, or reading *Walden* by Thoreau. Such activities give you time to reflect and assess. They let you reset and make sure you're on the path you want to be on living the life of your choice in a healthy, centered, and moral way.

Ultimately, the spiritual dimension is how a person defines how he or she wants to live and what a relationship with God looks like.

These three components of religion can mutually coexist, or stand alone. You'll need to think about what mix of each bucket you what in your life and when. You can be spiritual without ever attending a mosque or church. You can attend temple regularly and not have cultural or spiritual dimensions in your life. You can even embrace the cultural elements of religion, as many people do, and jettison the spiritual and ceremonial. The choice is yours and the challenge is to develop your own philosophy.

I will politely suggest you think about spirituality and discover what role that will play in your life—that really is the foundation of religion and will help you find greater and deeper happiness and fulfillment. I'm not sure religion can exclusively be defined by the cultural. The formal ceremonial acts and the cultural acts of religion provide memories, glue, and context for the spiritual. I think it all works together, but not embracing the spiritual might be misguided.

DON'T DO UNETHICAL THINGS

There are devoted religious people, in all religions, who are zealots; they attend prayer services daily or weekly and live immoral lives—committing unethical acts and crimes. They're ceremonially religious, but appear not to have a spiritual center.

Additionally, some people find religious spirituality through meditation or communing with nature and eschewing ceremonial and formal religion.

There's no correct balance or formula here, other than don't do unethical things. Most of us inherently know right from wrong (though we often veer off course). Being hyper-religious cannot erase the wrong in our lives.

BE OF SERVICE

Going back to the Golden Rule, part of being a good person is altruism, doing for others and providing service for others.

John Kenny works with people struggling with addiction. He considers his role in these relationships as a true act of service; he's helping others without expectation of anything in return. Knowing that he's helping and serving others, John feels positive and good.

The same elements of altruism, extending yourself to others, can be found in faith. Helping others, without thought of payment, is part of the key to happiness, according to Eric Polokoff. It's one of the ways you increase the satisfaction in your life and feel better about yourself.

The Dalai Lama, spiritual leader of Tibet and Nobel Peace Prize laureate, recently wrote an article in *The New York Times* highlighting the need for service in our lives:

> "In one shocking experiment, researchers found that senior citizens who didn't feel useful to others were nearly three times as likely to die prematurely as those who did feel useful. This speaks to a broader human truth: We all need to be needed. Being 'needed' does not entail selfish pride or unhealthy attachment to the worldly esteem of others. Rather, it consists of a natural human hunger to serve our fellow men and women." [33]

The Dalai Lama is asserting that serving others is not only something that can make you feel good, it's also good for your health!

FAITH

When it comes to faith, Eric Polokoff offered some other wonderful insights and perspectives:

- Faith asks you to stretch morally and offers some sense that you're doing intrinsically good, that you're benefiting other people's lives.

- Being faith-oriented is an advantage in dealing with life's inevitable challenges and helps keep you grounded and sane.

- Being part of a faith-based religious community brings you together with other people. Not only does it create relational bonds, it gives you the opportunity to meet people you might have not otherwise encountered.

- Any faith community is a mix of people and brings you outside of your comfort zone, because you're interacting with people you might not be predisposed to. For example, in any religious group, you encounter older and younger participants, people from different educational backgrounds, and people with varied socioeconomic characteristics. This diversity is very helpful in developing mindfulness and character beyond the limits of your own small subgroup. By living and participating in a community like this, you're forced to move beyond yourself and those similar to you.

- Spirituality is about taking religious writings and applying those texts to being a good and empathetic human being.

- People who are faith-centric are just happier and more satisfied in their lives.

SPIRITUALITY

Some people turn to spirituality, or the connection with nature and the God within, as a way to find joy and peace. There are few, if any, formalized rituals or customs in most spiritual philosophies (as opposed to most religious traditions), but that's often what most appeals.

Spirituality is a rather broad topic. While I've tried to capture a sense of it, as it pertains to religion, I want to underline a few ideas you may find interesting, or hopeful.

John Kenny believes God resides in all of us and we can tap into that as we choose. He defines spirituality as being a good person, of having love and service at the core. Meaning that to be a good person, your intentions need to be positive and you need to serve others. It's hard to be spiritual if you're only doing things for yourself and not in service of others or a great cause.

According to Joe Smith, even if you aren't religious, and don't believe that you have godliness in you, you have goodliness, instead—a secular form of the same concept.

A divine spark, or some goodness, is what Willy Mac-Mullen believes dwells in all of us—the Emersonian idea that the divine can be experienced every day, within each of us. Another way to put it, there can be extraordinary located in the ordinary, and spirituality can be found in natural life.

I agree; there's some type of positive light or spark in all of us. Fundamentally, all people have goodness in them and want to do good. Sometimes it's just hidden and needs to be uncovered.

In the words of Henry David Thoreau (as Willy quoted), "I know of no more encouraging fact than the unquestionable ability of man to elevate his life by conscious endeavor."

MINDFULNESS

One of the more mainstream spiritual practices of note is that of mindfulness. In a loud and busy world that requires so much of us, there's probably no better skill than the ability to tap into youself, to get quiet and connect with what you think and feel. When you think about happiness in your life, it might be helpful for you to explore and embrace the concept of mindfulness.

When I was your age, mindfulness was not a concept people spoke about or practiced as commonly as today. Being mindful, as the dictionary defines it, is simply "the quality or state of being conscious or aware of something, a mental state achieved by focusing one's awareness on the present moment, while calmly acknowledging and accepting one's feelings, thoughts, and bodily sensations, used as a therapeutic technique."

My cousin, Judy Bernstein, is an expert in mindfulness and teaches on this subject. Judy advocates using mindfulness to discover what's right for you. When engaged in this process, learn how to attune to yourself and hear what you love to do, what inspires you, and where your curiosity brings you. Figure out and think about what you're doing that will help build your path and guide you. This will help you engage more deeply and find meaning and satisfaction.

Judy has gravitated to things in her life that resonate with her and mindfulness has helped her to be present in the moment and aware of her mind, body, and emotion. According to Judy, we all anchor on prior experiences and models in our lives. Many of our opinions, reactions, and habits are conditioned. We should be aware of how they were formed and consciously embrace or reject them, but not accept them simply by default.

I'm sure you have embraced many things, some positive and some negative, from our family's modeling. The key for you as a young adult is to find what resonates with you genuinely and not feel compelled to accept anything that's imposed.

Psychology teaches us that we each possess either an internal or external locus of control. This means you either believe your life events are internally controlled by you—you determine how life unfolds by your thoughts and actions; or you're externally influenced by the environment, and not in control. Judy proposes that by using mindfulness, you can get closer to an internal locus of control and have a greater sense of calm and satisfaction because you're intuitively and actively determining what happens.

WRAP UP

We all face failure, doubt, and disappointment during our lives. We question our purpose, feel the deep need for connection with something larger than ourselves. Many find strength and solace in the notion that there's something bigger out there, or inside of you, to depend on. At some point, you'll need to define a philosophy about what role religion and spirituality play in your life. There are no right or wrong answers. You have been exposed to religious education and have probably already begun to formulate some thoughts. When thinking about religion and spirituality, get to a place that works and fits for you. Don't feel that you need to model what Mom and I have done.

SECTION 3:
WHAT MATTERS MOST

RELATIONSHIPS

The word relationship is defined as the way two or more people are connected. It stems from the Latin word *relationem,* which means *a bringing back and a restoring.* Positive relationships with others center us, and are replenishing and invigorating in nature. You want to be happy, have deep and meaningful relationships.

While writing, I was constantly reminded of the role people and relationships play in our lives. Most of the topics in this book are about connecting the dots in relationships. Family, marriage, friends, religion, career, community, even health are all about relationships—those with others, and those with oneself.

One person I spoke with on this topic went as far as to say that relationships are everything, they make all the difference in the world. Ken Saxon suggests we think actively about what kind of relationships and environments are healthy for us, and to do as much as we can to position ourselves accordingly. Engage in relationships built on kindness, respect, and love—that's what Judy Bernstein believes we should do. And Andrew Roberts believes the secret to a happy life is all about people and building positive connections.

Andrew has spent much of his life focused on connections, on being involved in activities that are greater than him. Teams, professional work, volunteer work have all been about people and relationships. He feels a lot better collaborating and doing activities with others, as opposed to alone.

When I asked Ted Heavenrich what he would tell his twenty-year-old self as he began his young adult years, he didn't hesitate: *good relationships make you a better person and enrich you as a person.*

For Dennis Whittle, the single most important thing in life is the texture of your relationships—who you're close to, the depth and sincerity of those relationships, and the enduring nature of those bonds. In Dennis' eyes (and mine, as well), relationships supersede just about everything else; you should invest in and nurture those genuine relationships that matter most to you.

Many mentioned, when they thought about career, it was all about the people: who they worked with, their relationships, and literally being fascinated and energized by all the people they met and encountered, the stories they heard and witnessed.

Relationships—everyone stressed their importance, right down to the one.

Life is a team effort and we're all influenced and impacted by hundreds of others. People support you, advocate for you, invite you in, help you out, and make it all better. Isolation is risky and unhealthy and we're encoded to connect and be social. Things tend to be better when other people are involved and engaged.

When I think about the best moments of my life, they always involve other people.

HOW TO CARE FOR OUR RELATIONSHIPS

I've never taken a course on relationships and how to be good in them. We learn about relationships implicitly in life. We learn the ropes intuitively and through social feedback. It's worth thinking about, though: how you build and maintain relationships, whether you're a positive participant, or not.

One resource came up in conversation multiple times during my research. Eric Wisnefsky, for example, mentioned reading Dale Carnegie's *How to Win Friends and Influence People* several times. Ken Saxon shared that he, too, took a Dale Carnegie course in his twenties. Both Eric and Ken indicated that the Dale Carnegie methodology and philosophy have helped them better understand relationships, especially when they were younger and first beginning to make their independent way in life.

I, too, have read Dale Carnegie's famous book many times, the first time in my early twenties, while in business school. There are parts of it that I find a bit mechanical and tactical, almost in a manipulative way, but generally I find his philosophy very helpful.

We've talked about dating and marriage, careers and more, but if I were to pinpoint one thing that would make a huge difference to the quality of your relationships in general, I would say it's this: be deeply engaged with the individual when you're together.

I'm sure you have experienced time shared with people when they truly give you their full attention. They listen to you, actively; they're focused on being with you; they look you in the eye. You feel like they're really with you.

You probably have also been with people who do not listen; who look around while talking; they check their phone and otherwise do not feel present. This feels horrible, I'm sure you'll agree.

Be the one who's engaged and present.

PUT IT IN WRITING

Think about how you communicate with family and friends. Don't feel awkward or shy about telling family and friends you appreciate them (and what it is you value about them); apologize when you've done something wrong and move on; don't bury resentment or regrets. Communicating these things verbally is OK, but putting your thoughts on paper has a bigger sense of permanence.

You write very sweet birthday cards and I have saved them all. I try to write you a letter on your birthday, annually, expressing how much I love you, what specifically it is that I love about you, that I'm proud of you. I know you read these letters nonchalantly and they usually wind up lying around the kitchen counter for a few days (I collect the letters and have saved those for you). I hope someday, when you're older, those birthday letters mean something to you and create a link and connection in our relationship.

When my dad turned seventy-five years old, I didn't get him a traditional gift. It appeared to me that he had enough sweaters, golf accessories, and he no longer wore ties. Instead, I wrote him a letter, trying to express to him how much I loved him, what I specifically learned from him, and what some of my fondest memories were of him. I enjoyed writing the letter, putting my emotions and thoughts into words, and reliving shared experiences from decades ago.

When my business, ArchivesOne, reached a certain milestone size, I paused and wrote about a dozen letters to people who helped me get there. I thanked current and former team members, mentors, and other partners. I specifically thanked them for how they helped, offering sincere appreciation for what they did. Selfishly, I felt good writing the letters, and I think the recipients were touched and thought it was kind.

Tell those you care about and love how you feel, *in writing*.

You'll be glad you did and I am certain the recipient will greatly appreciate your thoughtfulness.

WHAT WE REGRET ON OUR DEATHBEDS

Dr. VJ Periyakoil is a palliative care doctor who has had many conversations with patients as they prepare for the end of their lives. The emotion and feeling she most hears is regret around relationships. People regret not fixing friendships or fully expressing how they feel towards family and friends.

In response, Periyakoil has developed the concept of writing a last letter to help patients get closure and have an opportunity to express emotions.[34] What a wonderful idea and practice.

I think the concept of a last letter is super, but I'm not waiting until I am old and ill—and neither should you. (This book is one long letter to you, Jake, and Leah.) If at all possible, it's far superior to write these letters and express your feelings and emotions when healthy.

STRONG RELATIONSHIPS = HAPPIER AND MORE SUCCESSFUL

Again, our very happiness, health, and success ride on our ability to form deep relationships.

In the famous Harvard Grant Study, George Vaillant—the program's director for several decades—attempted to discover patterns of happiness and life satisfaction. Following several hundred men over seventy-five years of age, the research draws a link between the warmth of one's relationships and health and happiness in old age. Vaillant also points out that those participants who ranked highest in warm relationships earned significantly more than those who ranked the lowest in peak earning years.

I'm certainly not advocating warm relationships for commercial gain, but it's a quantitative indicator.

Vaillant further notes that positive parental relationships in childhood reduces the risk of dementia, decreases anxiety, and increases overall life satisfaction at seventy-five. Meaning, if you felt loved and nurtured in childhood, old age will be kinder to you, as well.

Vaillant reduces the study, and the tens of millions of dollars invested into it, to one simple conclusion: happiness is love. Relationships matter in every way.

WRAP UP

At different times of your life, different forms of relationships will be more or less important. When you're younger, friends might be primary for you; as you get a bit older, your marriage and family will likely be most important. Regardless of which relationships you're most focused on, life is all about connectivity and people. Let's look at some of these key relationships that will bring great joy and satisfaction in your life.

FAMILY

Family is crucial in life. You cannot select your family, but they're forever. Our nuclear family has deep-shared experiences and a common set of values. Those bonds, those relationships, will not be replaced no matter how close you are with non-family members.

When you're a young adult you might be very self-focused as you figure out a bunch of things in your life. This is normal; you're going through a lot of exciting stages and changes. Try to keep your family in mind though. It doesn't take a lot of effort to send an email or text or even a throwback phone call. You'll be amazed at how your family will appreciate your communication.

SIBLINGS

I know that sometimes siblings can be a challenge. But these people will be with you forever; they're some of the few people you can, hopefully, unconditionally trust. Your siblings have a special place in your life. Together, you can make fun of Mom and me, and get all the jokes.

When I was a young child I would bicker endlessly with my sister, Jennifer. Most of the quarreling was over silly things like who had more space in the backseat of a car on a long drive.

Sometimes I see meaningless conflict amongst you, Jake, and Leah; of course, it's just normal. My relationship with Jennifer has evolved and I now value and cherish her friendship, opinions, and perspectives. It's a treat to see her and her family and speak on the telephone.

As you grow older, your relationships with Jake and Leah will change and become closer and more meaningful, just as mine has with Jennifer. You'll diverge in interests, geography, and careers, but you'll always have each other as trusted confidants and loved family members.

When Dennis Whittle was younger, he didn't fully understand the importance of family. Specifically, he didn't comprehend his role as an older brother. He didn't realize the extent to which his younger siblings looked up to him, consciously or not, as a role model, and the degree to which they needed him to pay attention to, spend time, and be intimate with them. When I first heard this, I was confused. What could be more intimate than a sibling? Upon reflection, I think I understand what Dennis was getting at. You can have a sibling, but not be close. You can have a sibling and express disdain towards their actions and being. You can have a sibling and view them as a competitor or rival.

Sometimes I see elements of this behavior in you, Jake, and Leah. I hope the three of you remember that siblings are special and should be embraced, trusted, and nurtured. Very few relationships in life are truly lifelong. Your siblings are there for the entire program.

WHEN THINGS GO SIDEWAYS

When I was thirty-four years old, I had to go to the hospital.

When I arrived at the emergency room, in an ambulance, I was quickly examined by a SWAT team of doctors and informed I'd had a heart attack. It was pretty bizarre. I wound up having a slew of tests done in two hospitals over a week, which is a considerable amount of time to be hospitalized. It turned out that I didn't have a heart attack, but rather a rare virus called myocarditis.

While in the hospital, my dad visited me every single day to say hello and help me pass the time. That experience revealed to me the importance of family—especially when things go sideways. They're the ones who show up, call, or ask to help.

Friends are wonderful companions and certainly important, but sometimes the room thins out pretty quickly when you hit a rough patch or truly need help. Family is a foundation in your life and you should do your best to maintain and nurture those relationships.

GET YOUR PRIORITIES STRAIGHT

My dad recently shared the importance of family in an anecdote. My mom and dad were planning on attending a party at a friend's house. Several days before the party, a family issue popped up and my parents politely let the party host know they would be unable to attend the party as previously planned. The host was angry and thought it was rude that my parents cancelled with only two days' notice. My dad responded by informing their friend that his family came first; though sorry they had to cancel, their priority was with family.

My dad is about to turn eighty and has some perspective. He recognizes that friends are indeed important, particularly when you're younger. But family is enduring and permanent and really should be a priority.

When Brad Hutensky was in his twenties, he was very focused on his friends and often left his family to do things with them. At that point in his life, his friends were the center for him. Some of these important, close friends at the time are people he no longer speaks with or sees. Nothing bad happened, their lives just moved in different directions.

A parent himself, now, Brad believes that family is extraordinarily important. He tries to spend as much time as possible with his parents, who are in their eighties, because he knows the time is limited, and his parents will appreciate it. He also wants to model this behavior for his children.

Time is a gift for everybody. Make sure you're giving it to the right people.

THE DINNER RITUAL

I have so many fantastic memories of our family and the different stages of its evolution. Each child changed the dynamic, and each personality developed and matured over time. One of my fondest and simplest memories of our family is our dinner ritual: each one of us would share something that made us happy, something we were grateful for. It may seem rare, now—with school, soccer, tennis, skiing, gymnastics, and the general hecticness of life—but we used to do this so often when you were younger.

When we do gather for a family dinner, I truly enjoy hearing what made everybody happy that day or what made you all grateful. I feel like this is a simple and easy way to bring positivity and appreciation into our lives, while also sharing something that occurred in our days. Sometimes, people would be silly and sometimes there were genuine reflections and thoughtfulness.

I hope these moments helped you understand what was going on in each of our lives, how we all were feeling. Perhaps you will continue this dinner tradition or invent your own family rituals.

THE INDEPENDENCE BALANCE

Although your family is important and should be a central part of your life, you need to have some independence as a young adult. You'll need to form your own philosophies and ideas; while I think your family will influence them, your family cannot suffocate you. Close familial relationships are positive, but smothering relationships will not be beneficial.

My mom grew up in a tight-knit family that lived in close proximity to each other. At times, she felt she needed to break away to find independence. Additionally, my mom thought family could not be her only frame of reference.

Note, this doesn't diminish the importance of family, it just acknowledges that it's one perspective and voice as you develop, and it's not always the best or even the right perspective. So, while you should keep family at the core, you need to balance that with your own independence, especially as you figure out who you are.

PARENTS ARE PEOPLE TOO

Dennis Whittle did not fully view his mother as a human being until later in life, particularly as she approached her death.

Of course, his mom was a human being; but sometimes we fail to see those family members who are closest to us as actual people with their own stories, dreams, failures, and triumphs.

Sometimes a parent can be viewed as the cook, the chauffer, the cleaner upper, and the coach. And while being a parent is wonderful, a parent is a person beyond the cook, the chauffeur, the cleaner upper, and the coach. We, too, have all the struggles and joys you experience. We were all young once, with lives ahead of us. So remember: all parents have experienced what you have experienced; they're people unto themselves, outside of the parental role. This experience, and our love for you, is what makes us excellent advisors.

WRAP UP

You'll experience challenges in your life because they're inevitable. Health issues, relationship or marital issues, financial issues, career setbacks—it all happens. Your family is the core resource for you in these situations to provide you with advice, help, support, a listening ear, and—most importantly—unconditional love. Your family, who is so proximate to you that they at times can be invisible in a way, are people too. Don't take your siblings or any family member for granted and be sensitive to their dreams and stories. A healthy, intact family is something that's special and a true gift and blessing. Don't assume it's permanent or a given. Take time to invest in and relish your family.

FRIENDS

Like family, friends make your life rich; they fill it with texture. Life would be lonely and empty without the warm support and embrace of true friends.

As I mentioned in the very first chapter, you're in that wonderful part of your life where you're building friendships and gathering people into your life. (As you get older, this can become more challenging to do.) While you're in high school, college, graduate school, and the early career stages, people flood into your life—new and different individuals surround you each year.

You also have the benefit of being with people every day for long periods of time, allowing you to build deep and meaningful interaction effortlessly. Furthermore, you're somewhat carefree, you don't have large responsibilities elsewhere. This is just about the perfect combination for making deep, genuine, and lasting friendships. You'll see people in many different lights and have the opportunity and privilege of getting to know them intimately. This is a special time.

I'll say it again: inevitably, we all encounter hurdles and

roadblocks in life. That's just the way it is. You'll experience failure academically, professionally, personally. You'll encounter health issues, and romantic pain. You'll experience financial challenges, and bad luck. Nobody is immune. The key to weathering these impending storms is to invest in and cultivate meaningful friendships. Yes, you'll bank on family first and foremost, but friends will also provide you with a support system and an emotional cushion when you need it most.

Part of creating meaningful friendships is by being a good friend and being available when your friends need you. Friendship is a reciprocal proposition. People tend to model behavior: if you're not a good friend, that will reflect back to you; if you are a good friend, you'll enjoy that reciprocation. We get what we give.

You'll see that building and maintaining friendships takes time, effort, and commitment. Relationships like these are not a given.

Real friendships are enduring and can transcend time, distance, and context. They're based on mutual care, respect, and love. They can persist when one party has a setback or another has a great success. Real friends do not disappear when a person experiences something bad. Real friends are not jealous when someone has a great win; they're happy and proud.

CHOOSING YOUR FRIENDS

In some ways, making friendships while you're in college will seem completely organic, which is one of the reasons I touched on the subject in that first chapter. A teammate from your soccer team, a roommate, someone in a common class will make for a natural friend.

I think it bears repeating: be wise with whom you share your time, with whom you build your friendships. Your friends certainly do not have to be exactly like you—it's super if they're not; it gives you exposure to different perspectives. Just make sure their values are in alignment fundamentally with yours.

If you hang around with peers who do the wrong things, abuse drugs and alcohol for example (think of Gordie and that frat party), you're more likely to slip into that lifestyle. There will be some desire to conform to your group and you might be more likely to veer away from your values and core beliefs. This is the very reason I encourage you to take your own path, to eschew what everybody else thinks you should do. Peer pressure can pull you in a negative direction, and plenty of evidence indicates, human nature being what it is, we tend to mimic our friends' behavior.

So, it's fantastic to have a diverse group of friends, just make sure the friends you choose to be with are people who make smart choices and with whose decisions you feel comfortable.

GENUINE FRIENDS

Genuine friends are those you can call in the middle of the night for help or advice. They take an active interest in you and your family. They're the ones you can truly rely on.

This type of friendship requires work and time. In other words, it's not always effortless or easy. History and shared experiences bind friendships, yes, but you need to devote energy to their upkeep.

Ronald Sharp, professor of English at Vassar College, teaches a course on the literature of friendship. He says, "It's not about what someone can do for you, it's who and what the two of you become in each other's presence."[35]

Despite Professor Sharp's definition, true friends often do amazing things for you, above and beyond the typical call of duty. In 1989, my friend from business school, Adam Berkman, introduced me to your mom and that changed my life. How is it possible to express enough appreciation for a gift like that? Adam and his wife, Elissa, have been true friends for over twenty-five years.

Not every friendship will meet the criteria of a genuine friendship, as I am defining it here. Sometimes it's worth considering what kind of friendship you have in hand, so you know how to prioritize them. Being aware of why a friendship exists can be important; assessing whether the friendship is based on pure motives, or on something else, is helpful. Joe Smith says, "It is important to know what people want in a relationship, whatever type of friendship it is." Sometimes people aren't really acting in a genuine manner and Joe believes it's important to know this and understand the reasons behind it.

Of course, not every reason for behaving in a disingenuous manner is nefarious. Sometimes people act oddly because they're too busy trying to please everybody. When Joe was younger, he had "a burn to make everyone like him or be happy with him." That feeling didn't serve him or his friendships well. Joe now realizes this isn't realistic, that he needs to prioritize those relationships in his life that matter most to him, starting with his family.

It's hard to have a genuine friendship with someone when you're not true peers or equals in the relationship. Generally, if you're paying someone for something, it's hard to be true friends, because part of the relationship is based on compensation. This doesn't mean you cannot be friends at some level, but it might not be a pure form of friendship. It's hard to be friends with somebody when there's an imbalance of power; when one person is clearly in control and the other is not.

Seek out genuine friendships, and nurture them well over the years.

THE LAYERS OF FRIENDSHIP

A *New York Times* article on friendship offers, "Because time is limited, so, too, is the number of friends you can have."[36]

This train of thought stems from British psychologist Robin I.M. Dunbar, who describes the layers of friendships each of us possess:

> "The topmost layer consists of only one or two people, say a spouse and best friend with whom you're most intimate and interact daily. The next layer can accommodate at most four people for whom you have great affinity, affection and concern, and who require weekly attention to maintain. Out from there, the tiers contain more casual friends with whom you invest less time and tend to have a less profound and more tenuous connection. Without consistent contact, these casual friends can easily fall into the realm of acquaintance. You may be friendly with them, but they aren't friends."

CONTEXTUAL FRIENDSHIPS

Many friendships in life are what can be thought of as transactional or contextual. A contextual friendship is one where your closeness to a person is based on a certain set of dynamics. Perhaps you live in proximity, or share a common activity; but the friendship changes when the context changes—somebody moves away, or the shared activity ends. Once again, these friendships are not bad; you just have to understand that they're not deep and genuine in nature.

Many business friendships can be warm, vibrant, and intense. Sometimes the basis for these friendships is the fact that people do business together and have a mutual shared interest in the relationship. You can be in a business friendship, where you talk to somebody daily for years regarding a certain project, where you share personal stories—but when the business part of the relationship changes or ends, the relationship changes, too. That's because what you shared, the foundation of the relationship, is no longer present.

What changes, is the question: does the friendship evolve

or disappear? If the friendship melts, it probably was not a genuine friendship at all. If it evolves, that's wonderful and the relationship is deep and can move beyond its original context.

Networking, which is done a lot in the business world, is not about being a friend. Networking is about loosely establishing relationships and contacts that might be professionally useful to you at some point. There's nothing wrong with networking and I encourage you to do it, but don't confuse networking with being a genuine friend.

Certainly some of the ideas I propose here could be useful in networking, but networking is more commercial in nature and not as deep. When you think about genuine friendship, it does not fall into the same bucket as networking.

I'm not being negative at all. Your life will have many transactional and contextual friends; they're in no way bad. They fit into their own silo. The key is to understand the foundation of each relationship—so you can separate your core, genuine friends from others.

GO BROAD OR GO DEEP

When you think about friendships, you need to consider going broad or going deep. In other words, do you want to have a lot of friends who might not be as close, or do you want a smaller, tighter circle of friends who are deeper and closer in nature?

Will Thorndike had fewer friends during his high school days, but those relationships were deeper and more meaningful. In college, he had a broader set of friends, but not quite as intimate. He keeps in closer touch with his high school friends all these decades later.

Several years ago, I read a moving book by Eugene O'Kelly, the former CEO of the global accounting and professional services firm KPMG. Sadly, O'Kelly died at fifty-three from cancer. It was between his diagnosis and his death, that he authored the book, *Chasing Daylight: How My Forthcom-*

ing Death Transformed My Life. I thought the book was very thought provoking with many meaningful themes. But one thing stood out from all the rest—how O'Kelly thought about the concentric layers of relationships in his life, and where he spent his time. Specifically, O'Kelly spent too much time on circles that were too far from his core. He wasn't nurturing the family and close friendships that were his inner circles.

O'Kelly realized at the end of his life that he was spending too much time on transactional relationships—relationships that were only about business and his professional life—and he missed some of the more important moments with his family.

Don't wait until it's too late. Think about what you want to focus on when it comes to your circle of friends: amassing a broad group of friendships (some of which may be more along the lines of acquaintances); or cultivating a smaller, more genuine group of friends. What you choose should match how and where you spend time.

MAINTAINING GENUINE FRIENDSHIPS

So, how can you be a good friend? There are many ways to go about it, but it boils down to this: make the effort.

When you're younger, you have frequent interactions with friends at school. As you move past school, you'll see time and distance can become obstacles in friendships. To combat these obstacles, you need to make an effort to nurture and maintain relationships.

Sarah Bowen Shea, for example, works to surround herself with genuine friends, so she consciously thinks about how she shares real time with them, not in the digital world. She writes notes and letters—with actual paper, ink, envelopes, and stamps. She enjoys letting her friends know she's thinking about them; specifically, she tells them what she was thinking, when they popped into her mind—and it's always positive.

Another friend, who asked to remain anonymous, is part

of a group of six friends, whose friendships date back as far as kindergarten. Some members of the group live locally, some further away. To bridge the gap, this group annually gets together for a multi-day reunion, without fail. These are the close relationships he believes are important.

This same friend, who's a bit older than me, also saved scores of letters from his best friend, written while they were in college approximately forty years ago. (As much as it might seem foreign to you, people exchanged letters before email, Instagram, and Facebook.) Recently, he returned those letters to his friend, since they are a type of biography documenting the author's life in college and post college. Keeping those letters for decades serves as proof of the importance of the relationship and friendship. Returning the letters is a warm gesture, which gives the author a time capsule to his life from a friend and confidant. See why I encourage you to write letters and share your thoughts and feelings in writing?

What they've all learned: be determined at keeping in touch—through phone calls, notes, email, photo sharing, even social media. (Although, I'm not sure showing up on social platforms is a full substitute for meaningful interactions.) A true friendship cannot be grown, or even maintained, by posting photos and pithy quips about your life to hundreds of your electronic acquaintances. Deeper friendships take more conversations and interactions than intermittent electronic bursts.

True friendships require expressing your feelings and thoughts in an honest and vulnerable way.

Here are a couple recommendations for keeping in touch with friends—when you think of a friend, get in touch. Do it immediately, while it's on your mind. Maybe it was something you read—a book, news article, magazine article—that made you think of him. Send a link, say hello. Maybe you were engaged in an activity you know he would like—maybe one you previously shared. Touch base, let him know.

You can call; if the timing's not good to talk, they'll tell you. But more than likely, you'll make them smile and bring a drop of happiness into their day. If you want to be less intrusive, you can email or text.

Geoff Dietzel is a master at lobbing a phone call or email saying something like, "Was just thinking of you and wanted to check in and see how you're doing." He's also teaching his son, Tom, a freshman at Fordham University, this important and thoughtful skill.

Geoff told me a story about one of Tom's hockey friends, Daren, whose dad passed away. Geoff urged Tom to check in with Daren after hearing about the loss and, not surprisingly, being a teenage boy, he resisted, thinking it would be "awkward." Geoff encouraged him to be a good friend and call Daren. When he finally did, not only did Daren appreciate the support and comfort, but Tom felt good about it too.

MAKE FRIENDS WITH YOUR CALENDAR

Don't necessarily leave it to chance: schedule interactions with friends and family members on your calendar. Some you may want to keep in touch with monthly, others, less frequently. They don't have to know they're on your calendar. It's just a tickler that prompts you to take the initiative to touch base.

Some may feel this approach is too mechanical or contrived. I don't feel that way at all. If you truly care about someone, you'll want to make that person a priority—so you need to make sure you're reminded and have the time to touch base.

Recently, I read an article in *The New York Times* about maintaining friendships over a distance.[37] The article highlighted the importance of friendships, especially for young adults, and provided some real tips on how to maintain valuable friendships when distance is a natural impediment.

In the article, Dr. Irene Levine, an expert on friendship

and a professor of psychiatry at the New York University School of Medicine, claims when young adults are in different places, with busy lives, it might be necessary to schedule call times to connect with friends, otherwise it does not happen.

I'm not sure the advice is unique to long distance friendships, because friendships that are geographically proximate need effort to thrive, too.

I've had several friends with whom I scheduled a recurring call or lunch to stay connected. There's something compelling about the calendar, and once an appointment is on the calendar, it tends to stick. I've heard people say that you care about what you allocate your time to on your calendar. If personal relationships matter, they get prioritized on the calendar.

Currently, I have a monthly lunch with my friend, Jim Ratliff. I always look forward to catching up and connecting. Keep in mind, Jim and I live about forty minutes away from each other—not exactly long distance, but without the schedule, months, or years, could run by without connecting.

MORE ON NURTURING FRIENDSHIPS

Go to those special events. Go to your friend's important events: weddings, birthdays, ceremonies for newborns. You'll be flooded with weddings and birthday milestones at certain points in your life. Try to go. At times, it will be expensive—periodically, inconvenient, logistically most of all. But if they're truly friends and matter to you, be there for them during their special moments.

Will Thorndike has tried to go out of his way not to miss the weddings and birthday celebrations of family members and friends. When you attend these special events you're literally expressing your commitment to the relationship and physically showing the relationship's importance and value. Conversely, if you don't invest the time and energy to attend, you're saying you have better things to do, that it really doesn't matter to you whether you're there for a friend or not.

When I was in my late twenties, one of my friends was getting married. I didn't go to the wedding because it was expensive to make the trip, and far. Not long after, another married in Panama; the timing of the wedding overlapped with my honeymoon in South America. Mom and I looked into diverting our return trip home, through Panama, yet it was very expensive. I missed that wedding, as well.

I really regret missing my friends' weddings. Those were bad decisions on my part, and I wasn't as good a friend as I could have been. Don't make the same mistake.

Share time and experiences. Doing things with friends creates and strengthens bonds and lifelong memories. I'm not sure that the particular activity actually matters, as long as you continue to do things together. Part of the shared memories and experiences are all the mishaps and fun that took place.

Refresh your experiences. Friendships need to be current. If your only basis for the friendship is a common experience that happened a long time ago, the friendship will ultimately atrophy. For a friendship to be alive and vibrant, there needs to be current common interests and experiences. It doesn't matter what they are, as long as you're adding layers to the relationship and not allowing the relationship to get stale, or live in a moment in time that has long passed.

Sometimes, when I get together with old friends, there's a bit of reliving what was long ago. I always try to keep the conversation in the current mode; because talking about what happened in 1985 for the hundredth time just gets old. Intuitively, I know the relationship cannot only be about what happened decades ago.

An intense shared common experience is a great way to launch a friendship, but it also needs to move beyond that one moment.

Be the catalyst. Be the one to suggest activities, then organize them. You'll be amazed at how people will appreciate it and how it will positively impact the relationship.

Be empathetic. Empathy is the ability to understand and share the feelings of others. Displaying empathy is a key part of being a friend—trying to put yourself in someone else's shoes. My friend Matt Guyer has been thoughtful and empathetic with me over the years. We've shared many rambling conversations. Matt has a wonderful way of listening and asking sharpening questions to challenge my thoughts and views. Matt is married with two kids and sometimes—when I felt like I had a thousand balls in the air with family, kids, health, and business, like I was running in circles—Matt could not only identify with where I was, he also displayed sincere empathy. It feels wonderful to be understood.

Be there. Be present. Not just for special events (though those are vital), but in good times and in bad. Friendships are about being physically and emotionally available. You cannot be a good friend only when things are good—and I assure you, things are never *always* good—because that makes you a fair-weather friend. When things go bad for a friend, that's the most important time to step up and be available for support, companionship, and maybe advice.

Seeing how people behave when things are bad reveals their character. Sticking by a friend when he's down reflects the true nature of unconditional support.

Additionally, when things go really well for a friend, be a fan and an unabashed supporter. Share in his success through your happiness and joy. Don't be jealous or resentful; be happy. If a friendship is strong and deep, it can withstand both good and bad things happening.

Listen. Part of being a good friend is just listening and hearing out what a person is thinking, what he or she needs. When you listen, try to actively listen with a nonjudgmental and open mind. Resist the temptation to think about what you'll say next; listen carefully. When a friend talks about what he's thinking and doing, try to reflect whether he's behaving in a way that's consistent with his values and principles. If your friend is veering off from who you think he is or how you know him to be, it might be appropriate and worthwhile to tell your friend that. I appreciate it when my friends tell me I'm acting in a way that's off course—like a true friend, they reel me back to my center. Listening is about truly trying to understand where your friend is coming from, and why.

Sometimes a friend just needs to vent or brag, and you just need to listen. Sometimes a friend will ask for feedback or advice, then you should share; but if a friend doesn't ask for feedback or advice, resist the temptation to provide it or attempt to fix their situation. Men have a particularly challenging time doing this. Listening is just listening, not fixing.

Do not judge. We all come from different perspectives and places with different experiences and values. This is why I wrote an entire chapter about remaining open-minded, resisting judgment. It's important to share, celebrate, and seek to understand differences with friends; but don't judge. We never know why people are landing where they do in certain situations—perhaps we would land in the very same place if we experienced the same. Try not to have knee jerk reactions. Friendship is about a lot of things, but judging is not one of them.

Treat friends the way you would your business. Brad Hutensky suggests we be willing to do things for the sake of a friendship, the way we do for business opportunities. As an example, it's not uncommon for a business person to fly from the East Coast to Chicago for a meeting or lunch in a single day. I've done this many times. "Now," Brad asks, "what if we were to hold our friendships to that same standard?" In other words, what if we flew from the East Coast to Chicago, not for a business meeting, but for lunch with a friend? How would that change the friendship?

Sometimes, I observe people being more attentive and invested in their business relationships than in their genuine personal relationships—I personally have been guilty of this. The calls that get returned, the best hours of your day, they should be devoted to the people who truly matter most.

WRAP UP

Having old friends for long periods of time is very special. Watching and sharing lives unfold, with all the inherent ups and downs, is fun. Life can be pretty challenging at points and having true friends makes the ride easier, more fun, and more enriching.

Put friends high on your priority list; friends can be hard to come by and easy to lose without effort or you being a good one, too.

MENTORSHIPS

As you move through life, many people you encounter will play a role in helping you excel. Teachers, coaches, your parents, friends' parents, people you work with, neighbors, relatives, and religious leaders will all touch your life in some way. Then, there's the mentor . . .

The dictionary defines a mentor as "an experienced and trusted advisor." Let's unpack that definition because despite being terse, it's full of punch and meaning.

Experienced – the mentor likely knows more than you, at least on some specific topics. Experienced also implies the mentor has perspective over time, something you currently lack, due to your youth.

Trusted – signifies the mentor wants what's good for you and only has your interests at heart—you can rely on him.

Advisor – as the name implies, is someone capable of giving you advice.

If a mentor truly embodies all three elements—experienced, trusted, advisor—he or she can be a very valuable person in your life.

Mentors help guide you when you're a novice or uncomfortable. Mentors can be a sounding board, a calm perspective when you're uncertain or nervous. Mentors can help you with introductions, which open doors. Appreciate the mentors you've had, and be on the lookout for new ones.

Of course, you need to keep in mind that your teachers, coaches, advisors, and parents can be misguided and wrong at times, too. We all have blind spots. So accept input with a mild dose of skepticism. Seek it out; appreciate what your mentors have to say—but consider it in light of your own situation. Then land where it's best for you.

MICHAEL'S MENTORS

You're fortunate to have experienced some mentors already.

Mr. Heavenrich and Mr. LaCasse have helped guide you through high school by navigating course selection, extracurricular activities, and the ups and downs of doing well and not so well. You've built relationships with them and they've gotten to truly know you as a person.

Jeff "Freedo" Freedman made a big impact on you in your middle school and early teen years. You encountered Freedo at summer camp and you admired his enthusiasm, leadership and energy. Freedo was the first person to introduce you to the concept of values, how they become your character and can guide your daily activities.

Avi and Jason, your soccer coaches at Soccer Plus, introduced you to leadership and developing a style that would allow you to better interact with peers and people in general.

It's been fascinating to watch you interact with these mentors and see how they have influenced you.

FINDING A MENTOR

Some of the mentors you've had to date have been part of formal and structured programs, specifically at school, where you're essentially assigned a mentor. That will not always be the case in life. More often than not, these relationships will evolve more organically and will not have a prearranged feel to them.

You should actively seek out guidance and mentorship at all stages of your life. I'm not sure there's a direct and easy way to do this. You cannot walk up to somebody and say, "Will you be my mentor?" It doesn't work like that; the relationship doesn't even need the specific label.

What you should do is express a willingness to learn from more experienced and senior people. You should demonstrate a willingness to work hard. You should follow up and keep a potential mentor abreast of your work and progress. You should check in periodically with him or her.

Building a relationship with a mentor is not networking, which has a very transactional feel to it. A relationship with a mentor is far more genuine and unconditional.

DUCKLING IMPRINTING

Will Thorndike, founder of Housatonic Partners, a Boston based investment firm, discussed with me the importance of mentorships—especially the earliest ones in life. Specifically, we talked about the phenomena of duckling imprinting.

Imprinting is the phenomena of a baby duck or chick becoming attached to the first moving object it encounters after hatching from its egg. It socially bonds with the first animal it encounters, regardless of whether it's the same species or not.

The first scientific studies of this phenomenon were carried out by Austrian naturalist Konrad Lorenz (1903 - 1989), one of the founders of ethology (the study of animal behavior).

Lorenz discovered that ducklings would treat a person as a parent figure and have a preference for the parent figure, above animals in its own species. He also discovered that there's a limited window of time after hatching where imprinting can occur. (Lorenz was awarded the Nobel Prize for Medicine and Physiology in 1973 for his imprinting work.)

Similarly, Will believes we're especially susceptible to our earliest mentors; that we imprint on our mentors. We pick up and internalize the teachings—both positive and negative—and philosophies of those mentors we encounter at the beginning.

Will and I are certainly not social scientists, but I concur with Will's assertion. I believe we all tend to model behaviors. If a mentor teaches us the right habits and moves, especially early on, they tend to stick and shape our views, philosophies, and behaviors.

WHAT I HAVE LEARNED FROM MY MENTOR

One of my mentors was Tom Bird. I met Tom through my old college friend, Bill Jalbert, who coincidentally worked in the same industry as I did (as well as Tom and his partner, Ken Saxon, in California). I got to know Tom through our industry interactions, and found him very generous with his time, information, and guidance. After building a relationship over several years, Tom invested in my business with Will Thorndike and Housatonic Partners. Tom eventually joined my board of directors.

Housatonic investing in my business, and Tom joining my board, were pivotal moments for me professionally and personally. I cannot even begin to describe how much I learned from Tom on a business level and on a personal level. Tom and Housatonic gave me the tools and confidence to prudently grow my business from a single-site operation into a super-regional business. But, as I said, my friendship and relationship with Tom extended far beyond business. Tom has shaped and influenced me on many personal issues, too.

My relationship with Tom was particularly well designed. Think back to the above definition of a mentor. Tom had very specific and tangible expertise in my industry since he had operated in it for several years. Tom was trusted because our interests were completely aligned, and finally, Tom was willing to be an advisor and share his wisdom with me.

I tried to explicitly learn as much as possible from Tom. Along the way, I learned as much about a general approach to life, people, and philosophy. Not only did Tom help shape my views on business—*think about fairness; think intensely about customer service; start with the end in mind; layering to build relationships*—but he was equally impactful in other areas. Tom has deeply influenced my thoughts about philanthropy, aspects of family dynamics, and how to think about life's many chapters. Tom is about ten years older than me, so I benefit from his experience in each new phase of life.

Tom helped me elevate my thinking on a personal and business level and embrace a mindset of excellence in many ways.

IT ALL BEGAN WITH A BASEBALL COACH

Mike Erwin is a fascinating and inspiring person as well. Mike went to West Point and received a master's degree in psychology from the University of Southern California (USC). He's served in the Army, been a professor at West Point, and started a very successful nonprofit organization called Team Red, White, & Blue, an organization dedicated to helping veterans transition back into civilian life. Mike is now focused on the Positivity Project, a leadership development philosophy based on character development.

Mike shared with me how important mentors have been in shaping his life. At West Point, mentorship is formally built into the system, but in other chapters of Mike's life, he has had to seek out mentors more organically. Mike found mentors in his grandparents, community, and church.

One mentor Mike encountered, who he imprinted on early on, was a youth baseball coach who had been a Marine Corp lieutenant. Because of this coach, Mike wound up playing baseball at West Point.

This coach had piqued Mike's interest in military service and introduced him to the power of inspirational quotes. Mike keeps a notebook of inspirational quotes that he comes across, that he regularly reviews. (Mike, by the way, believes in the power of inspirational quotes to build culture, to guide your actions and thoughts in light of how you want to live. They also provide a burst of inspiration, which is critical for high levels of energy and enthusiasm, particularly when the waves of the world can take you over.)

So a youth baseball coach introduced Mike to his career path; that helped Mike begin to establish some life philosophies, how to find inspiration. This coach also taught him the importance of reliability and timeliness with a Marine maxim: "If you are fifteen minutes early, you are on time; if you are on time, you are late; and if you are late, you are forgotten."

He offered these additional thoughts on mentors . . .

First: They're vital to your development and progress.

Second: Sometimes it's best to seek out mentors who are not necessarily name brands or at the highest levels. Those sought-after people might not have the time to fully invest in the relationship.

Third: It's important for you to seek out and cultivate mentor relationships during all chapters of your life.

FIND YOUR MENTOR AT WORK

When Mari Kuraishi , the founder and CEO of Global Giving, was a junior professional and was figuring out her career and life, she was lucky enough to connect with Yukon Huang, a World Bank division chief for Russia operations. Yukon coached Mari on how to navigate a work environment. She was already very talented, hardworking, and smart. Yukon coached her on how to communicate her thoughts and opinions in meetings, and he had her back. Most important, Yukon recommended Mari for a mid-career MBA program, which the World Bank paid for.

You'll want to be on the lookout for such a mentor.

YOU'RE NEVER TOO SUCCESSFUL TO HAVE A MENTOR

Jim Smith, the CEO of Waterbury-based Webster Bank, is in his sixties and is about as accomplished a businessperson and leader as I can imagine. He's led and steered Webster Bank for decades. So imagine my surprise to find he still has a mentor. In my eyes, he's so accomplished; he's beyond this type of relationship. Jim, of course, knows you can always learn from others and listen to what they have to say as you develop as a person.

Other people should not shake you from your core at this stage in life, but they can be very valuable resources and offer new perspective. See, mentors don't tell you what to do; they guide you and ask questions in such a way that allows you to benefit from their experience and perspective.

When Jim told me about his current mentor, Dave, I immediately assumed Dave was older than Jim, but that's not true. Dave is Jim's peer chronologically.

If somebody like Jim Smith, a successful person with seasoned values, can benefit from a mentor, we all can. And a mentor can be any age.

BE A MENTOR YOURSELF

Which means you can be a mentor to someone less experienced than yourself, today. Not only do we all need mentors, we can all be mentors, too. You can help and mentor other students at school, and they can benefit from your experience. Think about how much you have learned, developed, and matured in your four years of high school—think of the insights you could share.

I look at you and see the same person you've always been, but also a very different person. At the core, you're very similar to the young boy who once wanted me to chauffer him around, and I'm grateful for that; but beyond that, you know so much more. This experience and perspective can help other people and students who are not yet in the same place.

I'm not suggesting you walk up to a student and assert, "I want to be your mentor." That would be very odd. But you might be in a situation where a student asks you about experiences you have had, and you can be a helpful guide and role model. Being a good mentor will help you develop as a person, too.

VIRTUAL MENTORS

You can have mentors you've never met or talked to. Think of these mentors as virtual mentors. Perhaps you've read a few books by an author who has influenced you, helped shape a philosophy or point of view. That's a form of mentorship. I've often reread books I've found to be helpful and impactful; I think of their authors as mentors in a way. This is why I've included a list of recommended reading at the back of the book. Think of this list as a treasure trove of potential mentors.

ONE-OFF MENTORS

Even if someone doesn't evolve into being a mentor, you can always ask for help or a conversation. Most people will reply positively.

Mari Kuraishi, a prominent social entrepreneur, is often asked by young adults for advice. She will just about always give someone a thirty-minute phone call, because she remembers when she was young, and making her way in the world, how she sought out that type of guidance and direction.

I often get calls from aspiring entrepreneurs and I always take the call and try to be helpful with my input.

So, even a one-off conversation with someone who has a valuable perspective or point of view can be very helpful and impactful for you. The key is to politely ask.

HOW TO BEHAVE WITH YOUR MENTOR

Let's touch on how to be a participant when you are fortunate enough to have a mentor:

- Be respectful of his time. Realize your mentor is probably giving you much more than you can reciprocate. Make sure that you're not absorbing too much of their valuable time and encroaching.

- When interacting with a mentor, be prepared and ready with specific questions and topics that might be helpful to discuss. If a mentor has suggested that you think about or do something, do it.

- If a mentor suggests you contact somebody through an introduction, follow up and do it.

- Make sure you are always appreciative and grateful. Follow up with emails or handwritten notes. Share with the mentor how he is helping you.

- Keep in touch with your mentor. There might be a time when your relationship with a mentor changes because of geography, time availability, or a change of interest. Keep in touch even after this occurs. As you develop and mature, your relationship with your mentor can evolve into one of peers. This is fantastic, but remember, your mentor has helped you and you should always be respectful and appreciative of that, even if your relationship changes.

HOW TO BEHAVE AS A MENTOR

- Take an active interest in your mentee's activities and development.

- Ask open-ended questions that allow the mentee to talk and think.

- Get to know what's driving and motivating the person and think about how you can help them develop.

- Avoid giving direct advice. Rather, ask questions to help the mentee figure out answers independently. Your role is to help the person develop and be better, not actually to do the work.

- Make introductions and open doors to the mentee that might be interesting or helpful.

- Keep in touch and check in periodically to see how the mentee is doing and if you can be helpful.

- Actively listen to the mentee and do not judge.

WRAP UP

Having a mentor and being a mentor will make you a better person and help you develop. I encourage you to seek out and maintain these important and valuable relationships.

One of the most important things you can do with a mentor is express appreciation and gratitude.

You're still in the early innings of your life. It's important for you to keep in touch with your mentors as you move into new chapters in your life. This is something that many people find challenging to do, and often people let these important friendships and relationships attenuate over time. I strongly encourage you to not let this happen.

THE COMMUNITY AT LARGE

You've been very fortunate to be born into a two-parent family, with no worries about food or shelter. You're healthy. You've grown up in a loving environment with a supportive focus on education and self-development. You were born in a stable country in a peaceful moment in time. Unfortunately, there are many places in our world where this is not true. Be lucky. Enjoy the gift. Young adulthood and life is filled with serendipity and randomness. You'll see people who had much better starting points than you, and you'll witness people who seemed to get dealt an awful set of cards. Where you are is a pretty good starting point. Of course, such luck carries with it certain responsibilities . . .

You should consider your relationship with the world at large, with your community, and how to make them better places. This relationship, your attention to it, will help drive your happiness and satisfaction as you move through life.

If you spend too much of your time and efforts gathering things for yourself and not contributing to a greater community, you can feel unfulfilled and empty. Eventually you may realize you're chasing something that doesn't satisfy you.

As a young adult you can seek out ways to serve and make the world better. Maybe it's volunteering as a soccer coach for children who need a coach; or supplying soccer balls to a league that doesn't have the resources to purchase their own. Maybe it's using your language skills and working with families that do not speak English and need help.

There are many ways for you to be impactful; and you have a calling to serve and make the world better.

THE PHILOSOPHY BEHIND IT ALL

Mom and I have taken you to Hyde Park, New York to visit the Franklin Delano Roosevelt Presidential Library and Museum. FDR changed the course of our country and lifted us from some of our darkest days during the Great Depression. Despite, or maybe because of, his privileged and patrician upbringing, FDR developed policies and exhibited a true disposition for serving and making the world better, especially for those who needed it the most.

The very first thing that greets you as you enter the presidential museum is a wall-size image of FDR smiling, his pince nez eyeglasses perched on his nose. Beneath the image are these words: *The test of our progress is not whether we add more to the abundance of those who have much; it is whether we provide enough to those who have too little.*

It echoes the cornerstone principle of the Jewish religion, *Tikkun Olam*, or perfecting or repairing the world—making it a better place.

Your high school's motto is another example: *"Non ut sibi ministretur sed ut minister,"* which translates from Latin as *not to be served, but to serve.* Again, making the world a better place.

The underlying principle, philosophy, behind FDR, *Tikkun Olam*, and your high school motto is this: you can always help and serve others and make your community a better place.

WHAT YOU CAN DO

You have the ability to make the world a better place and to serve others in a number of ways; here are a few things to get you started:

- Choose to make service a core part of your life by selecting a profession that's dedicated to service and improvement, like being a doctor or teacher.

- Use some of your spare time to volunteer.

- Provide money to causes that need resources to execute on their mission.

- Use your time, intellect, and capital to positively impact your community. Any combination of these three resources matter and are important, but if you can harness all three concurrently, you might actually make a difference in a targeted project.

There are many ways to serve. I'll give you some real-life specifics to help you see what is possible.

THINK BIG

Tom Bird has found a path where he combines his financial, entrepreneurial, and philanthropic skills by investing in and supporting organizations that have a defined social purpose. Tom's providing capital to organizations that might not otherwise have access to capital, to do good things. Tom's using his operating skills as a mentor and guide to help these organizations grow and thrive.

Mari Kuraishi and Dennis Whittle have dedicated their careers to service and making the world better: first, by working at the World Bank, and then by taking the entrepreneurial risk of founding GlobalGiving to do good. (Risk means they stood to lose any money they sunk into the project.) Mari and Dennis are bright, creative, and talented. They could use their energies in self-oriented ways, but have chosen to focus on improving the lives of people around the globe who have less and are not as fortunate. I would imagine this is very satisfying.

IT DOESN'T HAVE TO BE BIG

When you think of making the world better, try to think big and small. There are endless, unassuming ways in which you can practice *Tikkun Olam*. The simplest, according to Dennis Whittle, is to just be a decent person.

Many years ago, I was traveling with my dad while he was looking at a real estate property to acquire. One morning, we had breakfast in a local diner in a small town in the Midwest. During our breakfast, a person entered the diner in a wheelchair. This individual was enthusiastic and appeared to know many people there. He clearly had some physical and mental challenges and life was not the easiest for him, at least on the surface. When we finished our breakfast and were paying our check at the cash register, my dad asked the diner employee if the person in the wheelchair frequently came to the diner for breakfast. The employee replied, "Every day." My dad asked if he could anonymously treat the individual to breakfast for one month, then asked how much it would be. Some quick math was done. My dad paid the sum, and we departed quietly.

I don't believe my father was trying to teach me a lesson as his impulsive act of kindness unfolded, but this three-minute interlude taught me a few impactful things:

One: we can all make the world a better place for others, especially those who are not as lucky, in big and small ways.

Two: helping others is most giving and noble when done anonymously and without fanfare. It's a form of service and charity that's more altruistic and ingenuous. Of course, the person engaging in *Tikkun Olam* enjoys the benefit and feeling of knowing that he or she has participated in an act of service and giving; perhaps the greatest reward.

Joe Smith, who runs a successful regional insurance business and is also a devoted husband and father, has practiced *Tikkun Olam* in two impressive ways. When Joe's three kids were little, he made it a Sunday morning practice to gather up the kids and deliver them to religious school then take them out for breakfast, a neat ritual in itself. Joe also used the time with his kids as a teaching opportunity; he wanted to demonstrate ways to make the world a better place. While at breakfast at the diner, Joe would order up a bunch of egg sandwiches to go. Then, he'd pack the kids in the car and drive through Hartford, sharing the breakfast sandwiches with less fortunate people who were living on the streets.

Now, Joe is a dear friend, so let me needle him a bit and paint the picture of Joe and his kids rolling through Hartford in his tricked out, big, white Cadillac Escalade SUV, cruising along empty Hartford streets and doling out breakfast—a great sight. I tease Joe from a place of love and admiration. What a great message to share with his kids. How wonderful to try to make his community a slightly better place.

LINK YOUR PASSIONS TO YOUR GIVING

Joe Smith is an energetic entrepreneur and a former collegiate basketball player. Five years ago, Joe mashed up his skills and interests in a philanthropic way. With two friends, he founded a youth three-on-three basketball tournament in Glastonbury, Connecticut. The tournament, for kids in grades three through twelve, is played in multiple gyms around Glastonbury in an NCAA-like fashion. Joe's event attracts 500 participants and volunteers and raises approximately $30,000 for three charities: the CT Food Bank Kids Backpack Program, the Ghana Children's Fund, and the Glastonbury ABC House. Joe makes certain that 100 percent of the proceeds from the event goes to charities.

Joe's basketball event is an annual program and continues to attract young players and raise funds for charities.

What a great success story and example of how to make the world a better place in a fun, creative way that linked his interests and passions.

THINK LOCAL

Our friends, the Albert Family, are community leaders in the greater Waterbury, Connecticut area. The family tirelessly works on improving the arts, quality of life, and social service organizations. They're generous with their time and money.

One project the family initiated is particularly heart-warming. The Alberts decided they wanted a way to change people's lives locally, a pretty huge ambition. Similar to Joe Smith, they mashed up a few interests to create something potent and special. The Alberts support and believe in the mission of the Waterbury Police Athletic League (PAL). PAL is a nonprofit organization, which promotes partnerships between youth, law enforcement, and the community through educational, athletic, and recreational programs designed to encourage team building and foster positive relationships. This is done through programs that emphasize education and learning, as well as participation in sports and activities. The goal of PAL is to enable all young people, regardless of race, religion, income, or handicap, to reach their full potential as productive, caring, responsible citizens.

Additionally, the Alberts are long time attendees and

supporters of The Taft School, a Watertown, Connecticut boarding school.

Here's the mashup. The Alberts committed to getting kids from PAL ready to attend Taft, academically and socially, through summer school and mentoring programs. They made it financially possible for the admitted PAL students to attend Taft. I think you'll agree they have, indeed, changed lives.

HELP EDUCATE SOMEONE

In 2007, Mom and I established an anonymous scholarship at Colgate University to help two students from greater Waterbury (or Connecticut) attend Colgate. Each year we receive a letter from the two scholarship recipients and are continually amazed by what the students are doing and by what they want to do with their lives. It's really special to know that we're changing people's lives, helping them gain an educational opportunity that will hopefully be transformational.

TITHING

Ted Heavenrich also wants to make the world a better place. The first concept he mentioned was about being a good person, about having a moral bent to his life, and behaving in a way that conformed to his positive values and principles.

The second tenet he proposed was a bit of a throwback: he tithes. Tithing is a fancy word for giving a fixed percentage of your earnings to charity on an annual basis. Ted donates 10 percent of his pretax income to charities he admires. (I will emphasize that donating from a pretax number is the most generous approach.)

Third, Ted chose a career that's about service, teaching, and making the world better by working with teens and not only teaching academic content, but transmitting moral values as well.

Ted has really taken some specific action steps throughout his life to actively engage in making the word a better place.

YOU CAN NEVER BE TOO YOUNG

You should incorporate volunteerism, service, and making the world a better place into your life at an early age.

You had some experience with this while you volunteered at the YMCA in Waterbury, Connecticut, helping out with the youth triathlon program. It's neat that you combined a personal passion and interest with an opportunity to help and serve others.

Jon Hotchkiss told me a story about his two elementary-age daughters, Hannah and Sophia. They wanted to help some kids in another school who didn't have all the advantages and resources their school enjoyed. Hannah and Sophia set up a lemonade stand and used all the proceeds to donate to the other school to help purchase supplies for the classroom in need.

What a great way for young people to learn about making the world a better place and taking the initiative to do something. That's putting the concept of *Tikkun Olam* in action.

CHOOSE A HELPING PROFESSION

Talking with Eric Polokoff was interesting in many ways, but one element of our conversation stood out: his choice to dedicate his professional life to service and trying to make people's lives better. Remember, this is what Ted Heavenrich did as well.

Eric didn't always know he wanted to be a rabbi. As a young adult, he thought he wanted to go to law school, after living and working in Washington, DC, and being involved in national politics. These early career experiences pushed him in a direction of exploring how to help and serve Jewish people; specifically, he wanted to help build and maintain a Jewish community. This led Eric to jettison law school and pursue a path to becoming a rabbi.

Eric spoke about the great satisfaction he felt in helping and serving people in a time of need. Eric highlighted the humbling feeling of being part of people's lives at some of the most special and intense moments you can imagine: birth, marriage, illness, and death. The people Eric serves and works with in these defining moments often seek guidance, support, help, and answers. Eric kept coming back to the intensity of this dynamic and the notion that there is awesomeness to being engaged in people's lives in moments of joy and sadness.

When Eric uses the word "awesome" he's not invoking the colloquial meaning of extremely good or excellent—*that cookie was awesome*. Rather, Eric is using the word in its literal context of something being awe (a feeling of reverential respect mixed with wonder and fear) inspiring, magnificent, or wonderful.

So, Eric is serving others and is also rewarded by experiencing true emotional intensity when people are their happiest and saddest. Eric enjoys this part of his work—one he didn't have an appreciation for when he was younger.

In a similar vein, Willy MacMullen practices what he preaches. He has devoted his life to serving others through teaching. When we spoke, he teased me by saying that teachers teach for selfish reasons: they love it! He hopes that teachers positively influence students to go out and make the world better, that students will use the experiences they had, and the character they developed with teachers to do good. Teachers can leverage themselves and their resources to empower kids with the skills, the habits, and the temperament to lead positive and purposeful lives and make the world a better place. The best approach to teaching encompasses the heart, mind, body, and spirit—it's truly holistic.

SERVE IN THE MILITARY

Mike Erwin believes that pursuing a life of service is absolutely paramount to having a fulfilling and successful life. Mike has dedicated much of his life to service, first by serving in the military after attending West Point, and now by teaching and speaking about character-driven leadership in schools.

As mentioned earlier, Mike also founded Team Red, White, & Blue. This nonprofit organization is transforming the way American military personnel transition into the civilian world. Founded in 2010, Team RWB now raises over $6 million per year to support the organization's mission. There are more than 100,000 members.

Mike plans to return to public service as the next step in his career at a leadership level.

WRAP UP

The point is this: you'll find happiness and fulfillment by making the world a better place. And it's the right thing to do. There are so many ways to do this, regardless of your age or resources. Think about and embrace FDR's words, your school motto about serving, and the concept of *Tikkun Olam*.

CONCLUSION

Dear Michael:

If you're reading this paragraph, I won! You actually read the book and made it to the end. You might recall from the introduction that this book comes from a place of love. I only want the very best for you, and for your life to be filled with happiness, joy, and satisfaction—however you choose to define them. Live your life for yourself and nobody else. It's fully yours. Own it and relish it.

I hope this book gave you an opportunity to encounter me as a person instead of a father figure. I have plenty of faults; I've made more mistakes in my life than I can possibly count. You, too, will make plenty of mistakes on your journey. That's OK. But I hope this book helps you make a few less mistakes than you might have otherwise made; I hope it helps you make a few more good decisions, and avoid some of the worst.

This might not be a one and done book.

I'm positive that in reading it, some of the ideas and concepts explored just do not resonate with you yet. I hope I at least planted some seeds. As you move through your young adulthood years, maybe you'll encounter some words or issues that will stimulate you to remember something you read here. That would be a huge win. Pause, reread, or ask. Awareness and consciousness are enormous victories.

I am cognizant that at times I might appear to contradict myself in the book. This is not intentional and reflects that sometimes in life there is conflicting tension and a lack of easy and simple answers. This book is not an attempt to be a formulaic recipe so there are not concise and straightforward solutions. Many concepts are about finding your spot on a spectrum of choices.

As you explore who you are and what will make you happy in life, I hope you picked up on a general theme in this book: plan more, do less. Think, seek to understand, be deliberate, and then hope for the best. You will likely have a more fulfilling life if you think and plan more up front rather than hastily jump into something important.

To help frame this, I think it's wonderful to pop into a movie or restaurant without knowing what you're in for. That's a low risk, serendipitous event. The outcome might be great or poor, but who cares? But you don't pop into a marriage or friendship; you don't flippantly choose your values or virtues, your character or career. These take time and thoughtful planning.

I hope most of the content in this book is not fresh to your eyes. We've discussed and explored many of the topics over your two decades. This is really just a compendium and compilation of the endless conversations in which you have indulged me.

Relish and explore during your next four years of college. It's a once in a lifetime smorgasbord of intellectual experiences and opportunities to try new things. Learn to learn, not for an exam. By the time you leave college you should know who you are and how you are beginning to think about your path in life.

Be really careful with drugs and alcohol. They can change a life in an instant. In your twenties, develop the healthy habits that can carry you to 100.

The single most important decision you will make in your life is whom you will marry. Think deliberately and intentionally about this paramount decision. If you get only one thing in your life right, make it this decision. Most of your happiness will be linked to your spouse.

You can derive great satisfaction from your career, but it doesn't define who you are as an individual. It's part of you, but not all of you. Money and finances matter; but probably less than you might think. Spend less than you earn and diligently squirrel away savings as early as you can and as much as you can. Time is your ally here. If you check your spending and amplify your savings, you will, more than likely, be fine.

Relationships matter most. Family, siblings, friends, mentors, and mentees. People will make your life rich and joyful. Consciously think about how and where you are allocating your precious and scarce time and to whom. How you use your time reflects who and what you care about. I hope it's people that matter most in your life.

Figure out the balance and tension in your life on the resume and eulogy spectrum. Develop and know your values, mission, and goals. This will form your character and you'll easily be able to field the "who are you?" question.

Do not be scared to fail—because you will, and that's OK. Dust yourself off, get gritty, and persevere.

Discovering where you want to be religiously and spiritually can bring you a sense of belonging, connection, and identity that's greater than yourself individually. Serving your community will be your way of making the world a better place; and, selfishly, you'll enjoy it and feel great.

There's no rush and there are no magical secrets. Most of life is a tortoise-like endeavor. Looking for the hare strategy is usually misspent time and energy. You'll notice I keep a toy tortoise on my desk, to always remind myself of this.

Most of all, to figure out what will bring you happiness, fulfillment, joy, and success—cannot be rushed or achieved with shortcuts. It's a heuristic process and takes time.

You're in an absolutely wonderful and envious spot—the beginning. You have so much ahead of you to experience and enjoy. You don't know how lucky you are. I love you; and your brother, Jake; and your sister, Leah, unconditionally. This book is a gift to the three of you, but pales compared to the gift the three of you have given to me—being part of my life.

Zoot, zoot, zoot,

END NOTES

DRUGS AND ALCOHOL

1 Ashton Katherine Carrick, "Drinking to Blackout," *The New York Times*, September 19, 2016, nytimes.com/2016/09/19/opinion/drinking-to-blackout.html.

2 "College Drinking," National Institute on Alcohol Abuse and Alcoholism, December 2015, pubs.niaaa.nih.gov/publications/collegefactsheet/collegefact.htm.

3 "Alcohol Deaths," Centers for Disease Control and Prevention, last modified June 30, 2016, cdc.gov/features/alcohol-deaths.

4 "Impaired Driving: Get the Facts," *Centers for Disease Control and Prevention*, last modified January 26, 2017, cdc.gov/motorvehicle-safety/impaired_driving/impaired-drv_factsheet.html.

5 Maia Szalavitz, "The 4 Traits that Put Kids at Risk for Addiction," *The New York Times*, September 29, 2016, nytimes.com/2016/10/04/well/family/the-4-traits-that-put-kids-at-risk-for-addiction.html.

HEALTH

6 Cynthia L. Ogden, PhD; Margaret D. Carroll, MSPH; Brian K. Kit, MD, MPH, et al, "Prevalence of Childhood and Adult Obesity in the United States, 2011-2012," *The JAMA Network*, 2014, jama-network.com/journals/jama/fullarticle/1832542.

7 U.S. Department of Health and Human Services, "Health, United States, 2015," *Centers for Disease Control and Prevention*, May 2016, cdc.gov/nchs/data/hus/hus15.pdf#019.

8 "Morbidity and Mortality Weekly Report," *Centers for Disease Control and Prevetion*, November 13, 2015, cdc.gov/mmwr/pdf/wk/mm6444.pdf#page=1.

9 "Nutrition, Physical Activity, and Obesity: Data, Trends, and Maps," *Centers for Disease Control and Prevention*, nccd.cdc.gov/NPAO_DTM/IndicatorSummary.aspx?category=71 indicator=36.

10 "Morbidity and Mortality Weekly Report," *Centers for Disease Control and Prevention*, last modified November 11, 2011, cdc.gov/mmwr/preview/mmwrhtml/mm6044a2.htm#tab1.

11 "Injury Prevention & Control: Motor Vehicle Safety," *Centers for Disease Control and Prevention*, last modified July 5, 2016, cdc.gov/motorvehiclesafety/seatbelts/facts.html.

12 Aaron E. Carroll, "Closest Thing to a Wonder Drug? Try Exercise," *The New York Times*, June 20, 2016, nytimes.com/2016/06/21/upshot/why-you-should-exercise-no-not-to-lose-weight.html.

13 Healthy Sleep, "Benefits of Sleep," *Division of Sleep Medicine at Harvard Medical School*, accessed March 28, 2017, healthysleep.med.harvard.edu/healthy/matters/benefits-of-sleep.

14 Foundation for Traffic Safety, "Distracted Driving," *AAA*, accessed March 28, 2017, aaafoundation.org/distracted-driving?gclid=CO2otIPJvs0CFYJZhgodw34IGQ.

15 Harvard Health Publications: Men's Health Watch, "Optimism and Your Health," *Harvard Medical School*, May 2008, health.harvard.edu/heart-health/optimism-and-your-health.

DATING, SEX, AND WHO YOU MARRY

16 "Marriage and Divorce," American Psychological Association, accessed March 28, 2017, apa.org/topics/divorce.

17 Joan Raymond, "Single People May Die Younger," NBCNews.com, August 18, 2011, nbcnews.com/id/44122528/ns/health-behavior/t/single-people-may-die-younger-new-study-finds/#.VZcL6_rvg8.

CAREER

18 I first encountered the notion of a sentry post in a transcription of a lecture delivered by Irv Grousbeck at Stanford University.

19 Austin Schneider, "The Myth of Overnight Success," *The Huffington Post*, May 6, 2015, huffingtonpost.com/austin-schneider/the-myth-of-overnight-success_b_6819108.html.

MONEY AND FINANCE

20 Maia Szalavitz, "The Key to Health, Wealth, and Success: Self-Control," *TIME*, January 24, 2011, healthland.time.com/2011/01/24/the-key-to-health-wealth-and-success-self-control.

21 Mike Bostock, "Is it Better to Rent or Buy?" *The New York Times*, 2014, nytimes.com/interactive/2014/upshot/buy-rent-calculator.html.

WHO ARE YOU?

22 Richard J. Light, "How to Live Wisely," *The New York Times,* July 31, 2015, nytimes.com/2015/08/02/education/edlife/how-to-live-wisely.html?contentCollection=smarter-living&hp&action=click&pgtype=Homepage&clickSource=story-heading&module=second-column-region&region=top-news&WT.nav=top-news&_r=0.

23 "Reflecting on Your Life," *Harvard University*, accessed March 28, 2017, fdo.fas.harvard.edu/pages/reflecting-your-life.

BE HONEST

24 Charles M. Blow, "Donald Trump is Lying in Plain Sight," *The New York Times*, September 8, 2016, nytimes.com/2016/09/08/opinion/donald-trump-is-lying-in-plain-sight.html?_r=0.

RESUME VS. EULOGY

25 David Brooks, "The Moral Bucket List," *The New York Times*, April 11, 2015, nytimes.com/2015/04/12/opinion/sunday/david-brooks-the-moral-bucket-list.html.

26 Suzi Wetlaufer, "When Everything isn't Half Enough," *Harvard Business Review*, April 2000, hbr.org/2000/03/when-everything-isnt-half-enough.

27 "Character Growth Card," *Character Lab*, September 2015, cdn.characterlab.org/assets/Character-Growth-Card-8a9b-995138cfd2572a42c2d34ba958e340211cde8ba2a1e80ab44887f-b69c671.pdf.

28 Clayton M. Christensen, "How Will You Measure Your Life?" *Harvard Business Review*, July-August 2010, hbr.org/2010/07/how-will-you-measure-your-life.

HAPPINESS

29 Stephen Covey, "The Four Quadrants," *Quadrant 2 Associates*, quadrant2associates.com/Quadrant2.html.

EMBRACE THE PROCESS

30 Ray Allen, "Letter to My Younger Self," *The Players' Tribune*, November 1, 2016, theplayerstribune.com/ray-allen-letter-to-my-younger-self.

31 Daniels College of Business, "Daniels Concludes Voices of Experience Season with Ball Corporation's John Hayes," *University of Denver*, May 25, 2016, daniels.du.edu/daniels-concludes-voices-of-experience-season-with-ball-corporations-john-hayes.

FAILURE

32 Bill Pennington, "Cubs' Theo Epstein is Making Lightning Strike Twice," *The New York Times*, September 29, 2016, nytimes.com/2016/10/02/sports/baseball/theo-epstein-chicago-cubs-boston-red-sox-world-series.html.

33 Ray Allen, "Letter to My Younger Self," *The Players' Tribune*, November 1, 2016, theplayerstribune.com/ray-allen-letter-to-my-younger-self.

SOMETHING BIGGER THAN YOU

34 The Dalai Lama and Arthur C. Brooks, "Dalai Lama: Behind Our Anxiety, the Fear of Being Unneeded," *The New York Times*, November 4, 2016, nytimes.com/2016/11/04/opinion/dalai-lama-behind-our-anxiety-the-fear-of-being-unneeded.html.

RELATIONSHIPS

35 VJ Periyakoil, M.D., "Writing a 'Last Letter' When You're Healthy," *The New York Times*, September 7, 2016, nytimes.com/2016/09/07/well/family/writing-a-last-letter-before-you-get-sick.html

FRIENDS

36 Kate Murphy, "Do Your Friends Actually Like You?" *The New York Times*, August 6, 2016, nytimes.com/2016/08/07/opinion/sunday/do-your-friends-actually-like-you.html.

37 Bonnie Wertheim, "How to Manage a Long-Distance Friendship," *The New York Times*, October 20, 2016, nytimes.com/2016/10/20/fashion/how-to-manage-a-long-distance-friendship.html.

SUGGESTED READING

The 7 Habits of Highly Effective People by Stephen Covey

The Autobiography of Benjamin Franklin

Beyond Entrepreneurship by Jim Collins

Beyond Success by Randall J. Ottinger

The Book of Jewish Values by Rabbi Joseph Telushkin

Buying a Small Business by Richard S. Ruback and Royce Yudkoff

The Cathedral Within by Bill Shore

Chasing Daylight: How My Forthcoming Death Transformed My Life by Eugene O'Kelly

Creating the Good Life by James O'Toole

Endurance: Shackleton's Incredible Voyage by Alfred Lansing

Enough by John C. Bogle (all of Bogle's books are enlightening)

Good to Great by Jim Collins

Grit by Angela Duckworth

How to Win Friends and Influence People by Dale Carnegie

How Will You Measure Your Life by Clayton Christensen

Just Enough by Laura Nash and Howard Stevenson

The Last Lecture by Randy Pausch

The Millionaire Next Door by Thomas Stanley and William Danko

Millions of Souls by Phillip Riteman (your great-great-grand-mother's brother authored this book)

Missoula: Rape and the Justice System in a College Town by Jon Krakauer

The Outsiders by Will Thorndike

Prevent and Reverse Heart Disease by Caldwell B. Esselstyn

Race for the South Pole: The Expedition Diaries of Scott and Amundsen by Roland Huntford

Stumbling on Happiness by Daniel Gilbert

The Tortoise and the Hare: an Aesop Fable

Transitions by William Bridges

Walden by Henry David Thoreau

Wealth by Stuart Lucas

The Wealthy Barber by David Chilton

When Bad Things Happen to Good People by Harold Kushner

Winning the Loser's Game by Charles D. Ellis

For a wonderful, comprehensive list, check out Jim Collins' "Recommended Reading," online at: *jimcollins.com/tools/recommended-reading.html*.

ADDITIONAL RESOURCES

If you're wondering about which college majors earn what . . .
Otani, Akane. **"The College Majors that Make the Most Money**," *Bloomberg,* May 7, 2015, bloomberg.com/news/articles/2015-05-07/here-are-the-college-majors-that-make-the-most-money.

Or, where the jobs will be, irrespective of compensation . . .
"Hottest Careers for College Graduates," BigFuture, 2008-2018, bigfuture.collegeboard.org/explore-careers/careers/hottest-careers-for-college-graduates.

For things to consider before marriage . . .
Stanford, Eleanor. **"13 Questions to Ask Before Getting Married**," *The New York Times,* March 24, 2016, nytimes.com/interactive/2016/03/23/fashion/weddings/marriage-questions.html.

ACKNOWLEDGMENTS

Very few things in life are a solo act, this book is no exception. This project would not have been without the kind and generous support of friends and family who allowed me to do interviews. Many of my interviewees have influenced and shaped my life in some way. Doing the interviews was truly one of the most fun parts of the project. I experienced the luxury of engaging in deep and meaningful conversations. They were honest and reflective and provided wonderful content and perspective for the manuscript. Thank you to everyone who opened up their stories and experiences to me.

Here are the people who graciously agreed to subject themselves to my pesky questions:

Andrew Roberts	Eric Polokoff
Bob Galvin	Eric Wisnefsky
Bob Zelinger	Geoff Dietzel
Brad Hutensky	Jason Pananos
Charlie Saponaro	Jed Dorfman
Danny Rosen	Jeremy Zelinger
Dave Schnadig	Jill Hutensky

Denise deFiebre

Dennis Whittle

Jodi Wasserstein

Joe Smith

John Hayes

John Kenny

Jon Hotchkiss

Judy Bernstein

Ken Saxon

Linda Wasserstein

Mari Kuraishi

Marjorie Dorr

Marty Wasserstein

Mike Erwin

Mike Jackson

Jim Ratliff

Jim Smith

Peter Hicks

Peter Kies

Rachel Albert

Reuben Daniels

Rick Richardson

Rick Ruback

Royce Yudkoff

Sarah Bowen Shea

Ted Heavenrich

Tom Bird

Warren Adams

Will Thorndike

Willy MacMullen

This project would not have been possible without my book whisperer, Ann Sheybani. I connected with Ann through a friend's suggestion, and it was a fortuitous recommendation. Ann patiently guided me through the book's organization, content generation, preliminary editing, and then repeated the entire process again. Ann helped me understand the byzantine world of books and publishing a little bit better. My biweekly phone calls with Ann held me accountable and kept me on track when it would have been easy to dismiss this project as an indulgent folly. Thank you, Ann. I am grateful for your support and assistance every step of the way. You made this better than I could have hoped.

Amy Brueggmann is sort of like a kinder and gentler version of your junior high school grammar teacher. Yes, she did use her red pen generously in copyediting, but all in a way that made my writing, smoother, tighter, and grammatically accurate. Amy, thank you for making me appear to be a better writer than I actually am and for forcing me to remember rules from Strunk and White, which I read a hundred years ago.

Michael, Jake, and Leah, you were the inspiration for this project. Watching the three of you grow and develop has been a thrill. You continually surprise me, in so many positive ways. I want nothing but the best for you and hope this book, in some small way, helps you discover who you are—and build a life that's filled with happiness and enduring satisfaction. I'm certain there are many parts of the book that will not have meaning to you, but encourage you to revisit the book when more meaning can be found. I'm the luckiest father in the world.

Finally, I must thank my wonderful bride of twenty-four years. Jodi, I'm not sure how you put up with me and my quixotic projects—and this book certainly was a dream one year ago. Your unwavering support for this book, and everything in our lives, is the greatest gift you could ever offer. Thank you for enduring my constant chatter about the book and daily page count updates. Your feedback was always on target and helpful. You have helped me build a life filled with happiness and more satisfaction than I could have ever thought imaginable.

ABOUT THE AUTHOR

Personally, A. J. Wasserstein is focused on being a good husband, a good father, and a good friend. Professionally, A. J. teaches entrepreneurship to MBA students. Additionally, he is a private investor, with a long-term orientation, interested in lower middle market businesses and philanthropic organizations, where he can be positively impactful by using his experiences, time, and capital. Wasserstein was the President of Onesource Water, the third largest bottleless water service business in the United States. Onesource Water was sold to Water Logic, a UK based strategic acquirer, in 2016. Previously, A. J. was the founder and CEO of ArchivesOne, the third largest records management company in the U.S. He successfully built ArchivesOne into a super-regional records management company employing 400 people before selling to Iron Mountain (NYSE: IRM) after 17 years of operation. He has served on several mid-market boards. A. J. graduated from Colgate University and received his MBA from New York University. The U.S. Small Business Administration has recognized A. J. as the Small Business Person of the Year in Connecticut. A. J. was featured in the book, *Leadership Secrets of the World's Most Successful CEOs.*

Made in the USA
Columbia, SC
29 May 2024

36306839R00174